Poetry

à la Carte

- Poetic Devices
- Pre-Writing Activities
- Traditional Poetry Patterns
- Unique Poetry Ideas
- Projects for Sharing

Written by:
Connie Homan Weaver
Illustrated by:
Stephanie O'Shaughnessy

Edited by Dianne Draze and Sonsie Conroy

ISBN 1-59363-121-9

For more information about Prufrock Press products, visit our website
http://www.prufrock.com

❖ Table of Contents ❖

To my wonderful, patient family,
Samantha, Chad, Laurie, Eric and Matthew,
for all your love and understanding.

Introduction for Instructors

What is Poetry à la Carte?

Poetry à la Carte is the best way to sample a menu of tantalizing poetry ideas. Each activity is certain to tease the palates of both beginning and experienced writers. The lessons are presented so each one can be used on its own or combined with another lesson (for example combining one of the ideas from the entrée section with one of the patterns in the side order section).

The activities in this book are specifically designed for students in grades 5 through 8, but an innovative teacher in lower or higher grades can easily adapt the activities for his or her students. Each lesson presents objectives and lesson outlines that can be adapted to meet the needs of different ability levels and classroom structures.

> Poetry uses sound and rhythm to express ideas in a vivid, succinct way.

For many writers throughout the ages poetry proved to be an effective, creative, means of self-expression and communication. These writers not only wrote poetry but often shared their work orally with audiences. *Poetry à la Carte* presents opportunities for creative young authors to write, publish, read, embellish, and perform their work, and be seen and heard by their peers.

What is poetry?

Poetry is a form of communication that uses sound and rhythm to express an idea or emotion. It is usually compact writing and often employs figurative language. Poetry comes in many different formats, but it usually includes at least one or more poetic devices. These devices include:

- rhyme or alliteration
- rhythm or meter
- repetition
- symbolism
- simile, metaphor or personification
- imagery

Poetry can vary in length from long narrative poems such as Coleridge's *Rime of the Ancient Mariner* to the short limericks of Edward Lear. There are several poetic forms. The most common include sonnet, lyric, epic, ballad, ode, haiku, limerick, free verse, and blank verse.

Content or structure?

What kind of a poetry-writing experience do you want for your class? Do you want to teach them how to write limericks and then have them write their own limericks following the standard pattern for this form of poetry? Or do you want to use a more open-ended approach that gives them topics and formats that are designed to stimulate their own thoughts and present these thoughts in whatever format they find appropriate?

This book presents lessons for both teaching techniques. There are lessons that focus on the content or topic of the poems and other lessons that present a specific structure. By introducing various poetic devices, you give students the ingredients for making their own creations. At some point, however, each poet must decide whether his or her ideas are best presented in a haiku, a limerick, free verse, or some other format. The lessons in this book are diverse enough that students will get a sampling of various poetry writing experiences and be able to call forth just the right device or format to express their thoughts.

What's on the menu?

Poetry à la Carte has a wide variety of delicious offerings to make a complete and satisfying poetry experience. These items include:

- *Appetizers* - poetic devices
- *Soups and Salads* - pre-writing activities
- *Entrées* - ideas for unique poetry
- *Desserts* - projects that combine poetry writing and art activities
- *Special Seasonings* - poetry ideas for all seasons
- *Side Orders* - time-tested pattern poems
- *À la Carte* - ideas for sharing poetry orally

◼ Why is Poetry à la Carte a wonderful way to learn?

It is usually easier for students to write poetry than prose, because it is free of the normal constraints of syntax and grammar rules. *Poetry à la Carte* offers many wonderful opportunities for students to express themselves creatively. Through a wide variety of activities students are introduced to poetry in many genres, and because poetry writing is one of the best-known methods to elicit freedom of creative expression from children, they will find delight in their accomplishments.

Poetry allows students a platform on which to write more honestly about the feelings, emotions, and personal issues in their lives. If teachers use the activities in this book with flexibility, they will find greater success than if they were to box their students into strictly confined, follow-the-rule formats. Some of the less confident writers will use the patterns exactly as presented, and they will find a greater ease in their attempts at poetry writing. The more gifted writers will often ask if they can change the pattern somewhat to write the poetry in their own way. It is extremely important that teachers are willing to bend the rules slightly. By allowing this flexibility within the poetry assignments, you will be pleasantly delighted when the results yield a surprising amount of hidden talent.

> *The four types of writers –*
> * *naturally gifted*
> * *good, technical*
> * *occasional*
> * *gripers*

◼ Teaching poetry

Teaching poetry involves immersing students in rich language, exposing them to exemplary poetry by other people, teaching standard poetry writing formats and techniques, and providing them with hints for expressing their ideas. If students learn to utilize the different poetry techniques, their writing will become more fluent and they will find joy in this form of communication. In order to get the best results, your lessons should stress the following phases:

* **Pre-writing** is one of the most important and necessary steps in writing successful poetry. This method of brainstorming allows students an opportunity to lay the foundation that is necessary to build a good piece of writing.

* **Writing the rough copy** is a must for all poets. Students should never turn in a final draft on the first try. If students try to write perfectly on the first try, they will get bogged down with editing and proofing. This type of writing completely shuts down the creative free flow of ideas.

* **Present a polished product**. Whenever possible, students should type their poetry on the computer and add accompanying art to the page when they complete final drafts. By presenting writing in such a visually appealing manner, each person's work is validated as something of importance.

* **Publish student work**. Publish each student's work in some manner. Consider portfolios with attractive covers, journal sketch books, hanging pieces of writing on the wall or suspending them from the ceiling, producing class books of writing, placing samples in school newspapers, and submitting work to various writing magazines for youth.

◼ Four types of writers

Most students fall into one of the four writing categories. These categories are:

* **naturally gifted writers**
  These are the students who will write beautifully and well in spite of the circumstances, the assignment, or the inability of the teacher to motivate.

* **good, technical writers**
  These writers are often afraid to break out of the box or to take creative risks.

* **occasional writers**
  These writers experience some successes, but their writing is inconsistent.

* **gripers**
  These students hate to write and usually sigh and complain when a writing assignment is given.

Sadly, the largest percentage of students fall into the last category. It is not that they can't write, but that they think they can't. Teachers should attempt to reach students in all four categories. Even the gripers will flourish in a consistent creative writing program. It takes a great deal of motivation and preparation to lead children down the successful road to writing poetry, and it is important to know that students will become better writers only if they are asked to write on a consistent basis and in many different venues.

Using pattern poems

Pattern poems are wonderful for all students, because they provide a guide with set criteria to follow. Students can find a great deal of success and satisfaction with these poems, but they should not be locked into this type of poetry alone. The pattern poem leads them through the process, but still allows them to be creative. However, some of the more gifted writers often hate the patterns, because they automatically feel locked in or creatively inhibited. Quite often these students will find their way to the teacher's desk to ask permission to add a little twist to the assignment. It is important to give them some freedom in this matter. Don't lock them in the box. Challenge them to follow the patterns in their own way.

Pattern poems are wonderful for all students, because they provide a guide with set criteria to follow.

Poetry through the ages

Poetry dates back thousands of years, to as early as 500 BC when both the Greeks and Hindus wrote forms of poetry. While Greek literature declined, its influence spread, and by 300 BC Latin literature, which had its basis in Greek poetry, developed. During this time poetry also developed as a form of literature in China. Some 49,000 poems survive from China's golden age of poetry under the T'ang dynasty.

Sometime between 700 and 1000 AD the great Anglo Saxon epic poem *Beowulf* was written. During this same time period poetry in Persia and Arabia continued to flourish.

From its early beginnings, poetry developed as a viable form of literature in nearly every culture, but its content and form changed depending on the cultural and political climate of the time. Through the ages the content of poems and the importance (or unimportance) of following standardized rules has varied. For instance, during Medieval times epic poems combined history and legend and were presented orally but rarely written. By the early Middle Ages, however, the subject of poems was courtly love. During the Romantic era the expression of emotion was far more important than following the conventions of poetry formats. The nineteenth century was dominated by poets who often wrote about nature. During the Beat era of the twentieth century, free verse was the preferred mode and political and cultural criticism was a favored topic.

Examples of talented poets and exemplary poetry abounds. From *Psalms* the Bible, Homer's *Iliad*, and Cervantes' *Don Quixote*, to the more modern works of Walt Whitman, Robert Frost, Carl Sandburg, Shel Silverstein, or Dr. Seuss, you will find a wealth of examples that show different formats and topics. From this students will see that they have many options for their own poetry writing.

Poetry Pointers

☑ Always list many possible ideas before actually writing your poem. This pre-writing process allows for a pool of ideas for the poem.

☑ No poem is complete after the first try. It should become a series of several rough drafts. Keep polishing it until there is a quality product.

☑ Make the most of the words. Because poetry is written in a shorter format than other types of writing, more has to be said with fewer words. Carefully select your vocabulary.

☑ Think about what you're writing. Use descriptive writing to show your ideas and thoughts. Give the reader a visual picture of what you're trying to say.

☑ Let your thoughts flow. Don't stop to edit your work as you go. Write the piece seamlessly from beginning to end and then go back and make corrections or changes.

☑ Don't use rhyme just for the fun of it. The rhyme scheme must make sense and enhance the meaning of the poem.

☑ Don't just emphasize the sadness or despair in life. Write about a variety of subjects.

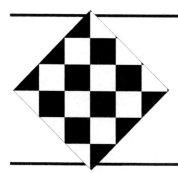

Chapter 1

Appetizers

A sampling of delicious poetic devices

Why Teach Poetic Devices?

In a gourmet meal the appetizer course manages to give everyone a taste of the greater cuisine that is yet to come. The analogy translates to the classroom, because it is also necessary to encourage students to develop a taste for poetry before they can enjoy the success of writing a truly good poem later. These taste sensations are called poetic devices, and they are the tools students can use to enhance their writing.

All teachers need to familiarize themselves with an array of poetic devices before attempting to teach poetry to children. An adequate amount of time should be spent practicing these devices with students. The eleven most common devices will be covered in the next few pages. Each one will be defined and examples shown, along with suggestions for student assignments.

One way you can use these poetic devices is as Appetizers of the Day. For a couple of weeks feature them on a menu board posted in the front of the classroom. Introduce or review a different device each day.

The devices covered in this section are:

- personification
- onomatopoeia
- rhythm
- repetition
- metaphor
- interesting language
- hyperbole
- alliteration
- rhyme
- simile
- imagery

Similes & Metaphors

◆ Similes

Similes are the comparisons of unlike objects or concepts that use the words *like, as, similar to,* or *seems.* This device is one of the most often used techniques in descriptive writing and should be one of the first lessons taught.

Examples

- Her hair is like a silk sheet.
- His eyes were clear as crystals.
- The puppy's tail was like a flag waving in the breeze.
- The book was as dull as a butter knife.

Activities

1. Write three similes about each of the following:

   The food at the fair smelled good.

   The river was pretty.

   The boy was smart.

   The sandwich was loaded.

2. Complete each of the following similes:

   Her teeth are like

   The chair was as comfortable as

   The needle was as sharp as

   His suit was like

   The shark's fin was like

◆ Metaphors

Metaphors are implied comparisons between two objects or concepts, omitting the words *like* or *as.* Where a simile would say, "her lips are like roses;" a metaphor would say, "her lips are roses." In a metaphor, it is implied that one object is another object. It is a stronger, more direct comparison than a simile.

Examples

- Her life was an open book.
- Her smile was an ad for a toothpaste commercial.
- His muscles were rippling waves of ocean currents.
- The horse's tail was a straw broom sweeping the air.
- It is the east and Juliet is the sun.

Activities

1. Using the four examples of metaphors shown above, ask students to write a paragraph explaining how the two unlike comparisons are connected or related. What images do the metaphors create?

2. Ask students to look for similarities between the following two sets of unrelated words. An example: noodles and toes are similar because they can both curl. Urge students to look for several creative connections for each word.

List A	List B
noodles	toes
blanket	spoon
computer	bread
couch	goggles
patio	lemon
ring	stove
drum	notebook
pizza	pencil
fingernails	vacuum cleaner
candle	basket

Personification & Hyperbole

■ Personification

This writing technique gives human characteristics to objects, ideas or other inanimate things. Examples of the often-used technique abound in classical poetry.

Examples
- The moon on the porch rail danced as if on a spotlighted stage.
- The tired old shoe felt lonesome and dejected sitting in the back of the closet.
- The rock observed the rushing waterfall as it came crashing down the mountain.
- The dandelion fluff ball cartwheeled in the wind.

Activity
Ask students to give feelings or human characteristics to each of these non-human objects and write sentences incorporating these feelings.
- a house
- an 18-wheeler
- a television set
- a can of hair spray
- a lawnmower
- a leaky rowboat
- a pen
- a computer

■ Hyperbole

Hyperbole (hi-purr-bow-lee) is an exaggeration. It is used for effect and is not intended to be taken literally. Hyperbole is often used in comedy.

Examples
- The odor was strong enough to kill a horse.
- He was so handsome that my eyes popped out of my head.
- Her biscuits were as hard as baseballs.
- The dog ran so fast its feet hardly touched the ground.
- His smile when he saw the gift was as wide as the Mississippi River.

Activity
Answer each of the following questions with an exaggeration.
- How tall was the building?
- How much money did the rich man have?
- How funny was the comedian?
- How cute was the puppy?
- How big was the fish that you caught?
- How pretty was the sunset?
- How angry was the teacher?
- How much did it rain?

Onomatopoeia & Alliteration

■ Onomatopoeia

Onomatopoeia (pronounced On-o-mot-uh-pee-yuh) is the use of words that sound like the sounds they describe. This includes words like *plink, bam, buzz, clink* and *boom*. This use of sounds enables the writing to seem more alive to the reader.

Examples

- The meowing of the kitten was heard above the sound of the television.
- The water faucet dripped and gurgled in the kitchen sink.
- The thirsty toddler slurped the rest of his chocolate milkshake.
- The clip-clopping of the horses' hooves could be heard in the distance.

Activities

1. List words that would demonstrate the sound/s of the following:
   - A bell ringing
   - A car trying to start on a cold winter morning
   - A finger streaking across a mirror
   - The sound of ocean waves crashing on the shore
   - The noises a person makes when he is out of breath after running a long distance
   - The sounds of animals in the zoo
   - The sound of static on a radio
   - The sounds of a motorcycle building up speed
   - The sounds of a baby bird in its nest

2. Give students the following words and have them incorporate them into sentences or verses.
   hiss, wheeze, drip, sizzle, buzz, whistle, clang, bang, squeak, roar

■ Alliteration

Alliteration is the most common form of repeated sounds studied in elementary and middle schools. To give a complete picture, however, it should be presented with the two other forms of repeated sounds, consonance and assonance. Students will likely use alliterations more than assonance and consonance, but they should be aware of these other forms of repetition so they can make use of them as needed.

- **Alliteration** - the repetition of initial consonant sounds. The purpose of this form of repetition is to create a pleasing combination of sounds. The sound can be repeated in two or more words in the sentence. An alliteration is a special form of consonance.
- **Assonance** - the repetition of vowel sounds. These can be anywhere in the word, not just the initial sounds.
- **Consonance** - the repetition of consonant sounds anywhere in the words (not just the beginning sounds). Examples: strive, live, love (the "v" sound) or time, slime, tame, same (the "m" sound).

Examples

- Mighty men make money out of movies.
- They cleaned until everything was spic and span.
- She looked up with quiet, questioning eyes.

Activities

1. Using their names, have students write alliterations.

2. Ask students to add to a list of common expressions that are alliterative – phrases like first and foremost, rough and ready, safe and sound, or blind as a bat.

3. Give students the beginnings phrases and have them add an alliterative element to make complete sentences.

Imagery & Interesting Language

Imagery

Imagery is the use of words to paint a picture that allows a creative image to form in the reader's mind. The writer chooses his or her words carefully so that the sights, sounds, smells, tastes, and feelings he or she is describing form vivid images for the reader.

Examples

- The sale at the dress shop was a feeding frenzy.
- The pep rally was a kaleidoscope of colors.
- The sunset was an explosive fireworks display.
- The smell of cookies filled the room with pungent cinnamon and tangy ginger.

Activities

1. Expand on each of these sentences to make them more vivid and alive. Write the sentences five times, adding one descriptive word each time.

   The house looked run down.

   The tree had new buds.

   The cookies were burned.

   The couch was comfortable.

   The lemon tasted sour.

2. Write a description of a major league baseball game or a rock concert. Use vivid words and all of the senses in this description. Turn the description into a poem.

Interesting Language

The use of interesting words makes the writing more attractive to the reader. Students should practice writing sentences that use precise, vibrant language to create sentences that paint pictures for the reader. Employing this device may mean that students will have to develop new vocabularies to be used during poetry writing.

Examples

- The scintillating table conversation provided a delightful backdrop to the ambience of the otherwise subdued restaurant setting.
- The obstinate siblings caused an uproarious distraction during the dignified church service.

Activities

1. Using a dictionary and a thesaurus, find words for in each of the categories listed below:
   - ten words that sound humorous
   - ten words that sound ugly (not dirty words, just words that have an ugly sound to them)
   - ten words that sound beautiful
   - ten words that sound like happiness

2. Take one of the preceding lists of words and write a poem incorporating all of the words. Note: Look up the words to get accurate definitions.

3. Pick a topic and do a mind web of ideas related to that topic. Use a thesaurus to find synonyms for these words.

Rhyme, Rhythm & Repetition

◆ Rhyme

Rhyme is using words with similar ending sounds. There are many types of rhyme and a variety of rhyming schemes. When using true rhyme, the last syllables have the same sound. For example, red-bed or cat-hat.

Rhyme schemes refers to the sequence of the rhyme. This rhyme is usually notated by letters of the alphabet. Whenever one of the letters is repeated, a rhyming word should be used. Some examples follow:

AA - The last syllables of each line rhyme. For example:

> *A little boy named Matt*
> *Received a brand new hat.*

ABAB - The first and third lines rhyme and the second and fourth lines rhyme. For example:

> *A child sat down for lunch,*
> *He ate a sandwich and chips,*
> *He drank his strawberry punch,*
> *And wiped the red off his lips.*

Activities

1. Look at familiar poems and nursery rhymes and identify the rhyming patterns.

2. Write a short poem for each of the following rhyme schemes:
   AABB, AABBA, ABCB, AAA

◆ Rhythm

Rhythm is the regular pattern of stressed and unstressed syllables in the lines of a poem. In many forms of poetry, this pattern gives the poetry its musical quality and provides a "flow" as it is being read. Writers who are attempting to create poems with a rhythmic pattern should read them aloud, listening for the stressed and unstressed patterns. If they truly want to create poems with standard patterns (like iambic or trochaic), they should mark the syllabication of their poems.

Examples

- iambic - da-DA
- trochaic - DA-da
- anapestic - da-da-DA
- dactylic - DA-da-da
- spondaic - DA-DA

Activity

Read several selections of nursery rhymes, lyrics to music, or poems that have a definite pattern (like Dr. Seuss or limericks). Have students clap out the patterns. Compare these examples to poems that have no patterns.

◆ Repetition

Repetition refers to repeating words, lines, or stanzas throughout a poem in order to give more emphasis to the lines that are repeated. It is an effective way to vary the pattern of the poem.

Examples

> *The wind blew her hair about her head*
>   *that day,*
> *And tried to whip her blue bonnet away,*
> *She cried "Oh sir, please help me along!*
> *I'm trying to get home, but the wind is so*
>   *strong!"*
> *The wind is so strong,*
> *Please help me along,*
> *As the wind blew her hair about her head*
>   *that day.*

Activities

1. Ask the students to write a poem consisting of two stanzas and instruct them to add three or more repetitions that contain some of the lines they have written.

2. Ask the students to locate ten previously written poems or nursery rhymes that use repetition as one of their poetic devices. Then have them present one of these poems to the class and discuss how the repetition adds to the poem.

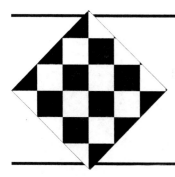

Chapter 2

Soups & Salads

Appetizing pre-writing activities

Before You Begin Writing Poetry

Pre-writing consists of activities that produce spontaneous, impulsive thoughts committed to paper. At times they involve simply listing ideas that pertain to the topic at hand. These ideas do not necessarily follow a pattern, rhyme scheme, or logical thinking, but they serve an important function in the overall writing process. They are similar to the "soup and salad" section of a menu found in any restaurant. They whet the appetite for more in-depth writing. They set the stage or enhance the desire for the entrée (poem) that is to follow.

Several pre-writing activities are provided. Some may be used as stepping stones for poetry writing, but others may be used as single brainstorming activities that warm up the brain and open the mind to more creative thought. Encourage students to keep a daily journal filled with random thoughts and their responses to the pre-writing activities.

Memory Journals

One of the most successful ways to get students to write is to encourage them to think about their own life experiences. It is of the utmost importance that students be given many opportunities to reflect upon the past. Thoughts of certain events are often stored away in their long-term memories and must be brought to the surface before the experiences and feelings can be used in writing.

Memory journals provide the means for students to chart a record of lifetime memories. These journals can provide a source for writing stories and poems about their lives. The following pre-writing activities about "memories" can be used as single, spontaneous moments or as the means to writing full-scale poetry. Teachers may also use these ideas selectively as daily journaling activities. Students should be encouraged to sketch, doodle, or write in any creative fashion they wish.

Topics for Memory Journals

- Memories of childhood
- Memories of family
- Sad memories
- Memories of accomplishments
- Memories of illnesses
- Memories of funny moments
- Memories of embarrassing moments
- Memories of pets
- Memories of family vacations or trips to the homes of relatives
- Memories of favorite foods
- Memories of scary things that happened
- Memories of special occasions and holidays

- Memories of bad weather
- Memories of the sun
- Memories about the day before
- Memories of beauty
- Memories of outdoor activities
- Memories of great surprises
- Memories of teachers
- Memories of friends
- Memories involving sports
- Memories of school
- Memories of current events
- Memories of good things
- Memories of "The first time I____."
- Memories of favorite clothing
- Memories of childhood homes

Metaphorical Thinking

Before this pre-writing lesson, students must first understand that a metaphor is a comparison of two unlike objects without the use of the words "like" or "as." For information on teaching metaphors, see page 10.

Have students select one of the subjects shown below and list all of its properties or characteristics (at least six). Once this list has been compiled, they should compare its components to something or someone with similar characteristics and write a poem showing these contrasts.

tree	fish
ocean	car
food	appliance
animal	river
toy	rock
place	toothbrush
gold or silver	noodle
shoe	rug
fingernail polish	fireplace
musical instrument	chair
amusement park ride	sidewalk
compact disk	can of soup
pencil/pen	desk
telephone	key
purse/wallet	money
summer's breeze	blanket
warm coat	

Example

A rug - its characteristics are:
    warm and wooly, comforting, offering protection, covering
Students then compare these characteristics to some other topic or object. In the sample below a rug is being compared to a mother.

Sample Poem

    A soft beige carpet,
    Warm and cozy,
    Offering comfort to all who venture near,
    Wrapping itself around the room,
    With outstretched arms,
    A mother.
    Protecting and nurturing the valuable floor beneath,
    For many years to come.

Option

You may choose to use similes (comparisons using the words "like" or "as") in place of metaphors.

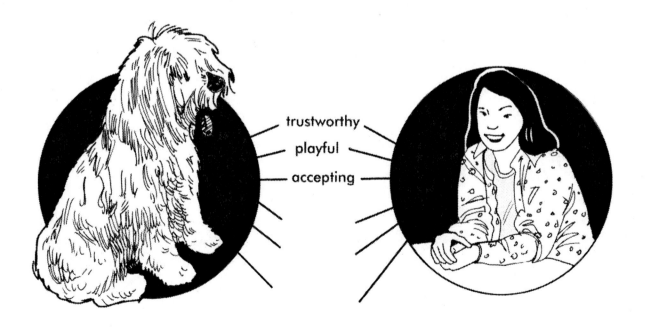

trustworthy

playful

accepting

Daydreams

Giving students permission to daydream is one way to unleash their imaginations. From these mind wanderings can come the ideas for inspired writings. They may daydream about things they wish for in their futures, fantasize about things they would like to accomplish, or imagine a better version of their current situation. While students will no doubt daydream with or without your guidance, giving them topics means you can direct their daydreaming so the results are ideas that can be used in writing. In the beginning, they should list phrases and words that would best describe each of the following situations. Later, they can use their brainstormed lists as the themes for poetry or descriptive writing.

Topics for Daydreaming

- Imagine your dream bedroom.
- Imagine the perfect day. What would the weather be like? Describe the setting. What activities would be going on?
- Imagine a dream vacation.
- Imagine the perfect job or career.
- Imagine an ideal meal that you would love for someone to cook for you.
- Imagine an imaginary dessert.
- Imagine the pet you'd love to have.
- Imagine your dream house.
- Imagine the ideal playground or amusement park ride.
- Imagine the ideal plot for a story or novel.

- Imagine the perfect rainy day afternoon.
- Imagine yourself doing something physical.
- Imagine the perfect beach scene.
- Imagine your dream school.
- Imagine the ideal teacher.
- Imagine a dream restaurant.
- Imagine the perfect setting for a get-away home.
- Imagine the perfect weekend.
- Imagine an ability you wish you had.
- Imagine how you see yourself in ten years.
- Imagine the ideal family gathering.

Zap Me!

In order for students to look at situations from different perspectives, they need practice getting into someone else's head and seeing an issue from other viewpoints. These writing activities offer several suggestions for ways to accomplish this task. Some of the ideas deal with people in a variety of situations, while other ideas involve the personification of inanimate objects. Students are challenged to think creatively and introspectively about these situations. Some ideas can be used for journal writing, while others can be full-fledged writing assignments.

Activities

1. Zap students into the following inanimate objects. They are to write words or phrases that might be said from the viewpoint of the items listed. Students may choose to draw a picture and include talking bubbles that contain the thoughts of the object.

   Zap, you're a…

   - A car in a garage
   - A potato in a sack of potatoes
   - A rock in a riverbed
   - A bottle of glue in a student's desk
   - A snowflake on a snowman
   - A pair of scissors in a drawer
   - Shoes in the closet
   - Tools in a toolbox
   - Food in the refrigerator
   - Items in a cosmetics bag
   - Laundry in a dirty clothes hamper
   - A necklace in a jewelry box
   - A fork in a dishwasher
   - A golf ball in a golf bag
   - A shirt packed in a suitcase
   - A chair in a furniture store
   - A credit card in a wallet
   - A prize at the bottom of a cereal box
   - A can in a six pack of drinks
   - A letter in a mailbox
   - A fishing lure in a tackle box
   - A burger in a kid's meal

2. Zap your students into the character from one of the following situations and have them write sympathetically from that character's point of view.

   - The horse in a horse race
   - Someone who is tormented by a bully
   - The teacher who students think assigns too much homework
   - The grouchy fast food clerk taking your order
   - The quiet child who walks down the hall not speaking to anyone
   - The principal of your school
   - Your parents when they are punishing you for lying
   - The telemarketer who calls your house
   - Your dog when you're talking baby talk to it
   - A person who is being ridiculed by his or her classmates
   - Your parent on a day when you are in a bad mood

Gumpets

Gumpets are based on a saying from the movie *Forrest Gump*. Forrest's mother was famous for saying, "Life is like a box of chocolates. You never know what you're gonna get." In this activity students are asked to brainstorm ways that life can be like different things. They must think of creative ways to complete each phrase.

Activities

1. Have students complete the following:

   Life is like a box of cereal. You . . .

   Life is like a river. You . . .

   Life is like a light bulb. You . . .

   Life is like a stick of butter. You . . .

   Life is like a birthday cake. You . . .

   Life is like a brand new puppy. You . . .

   Life is like a personal computer. You . . .

   Life is like a walk-in closet. You . . .

   Life is like a spaghetti dinner. You . . .

   Life is like a deck of cards. You . . .

2. Select topics other than life. Use the same format as shown with life, but use some of the following to create new "Gumpets."

   Example:

   Love is like a rose
   You never know how it will unfold.

   Sample topics:

poverty	peace
joy	fury
serenity	fear
love	popularity
excitement	humor
prejudice	sorrow

Sensory Cube

Keep a sensory cube or wheel on hand at all times for spontaneous pre-writing activities that result in good poetry and lots of good fun. Using the senses for pre-writing will enable students to look more creatively at the world around them.

Sensory Cube

Create a 6-inch cube out of cardboard. Cover it with brightly colored paper and use the computer to print out each of the labels shown below. Paste one on each side of the cube and add a picture or design for a more pleasing appearance.

Sensory Wheel

Cut a large circle out of cardboard, and paint or cover it with colored paper. Divide the wheel into six sections (like a pie), and use the same labeling system as described for the cube. Make a spinner or number each section and use the roll of a die to determine the day's topic. Hang the wheel on the wall for easy use.

Label the sides of the cube or the sections of the wheel with these words:

- smell
- sight
- hearing
- taste
- touch
- emotional appeal

Suggestions for Use

1. Using the cube or the wheel, randomly select a sense and ask students to focus on this sense. For example, if the selected sense of the day is hearing, ask students to close their eyes and listen to all of the sounds around them for a period of five minutes.

2. On a pretty day, go outside and spread a blanket on the ground for the students to sit on. Students should have notebooks and pencils handy. When time is up, they are to write all of the words and phrases they can think of to describe what sensations they experienced with the selected sense. They can then turn the words into a poem.

3. Students may also use all of the senses in one poem. Using all of the senses allows students to look upon life in a variety of ways, and the poem will have more depth.

Opportune moments for sensory writing:

- rainy days
- springtime weather
- thunderstorms
- snowy weather
- while music is playing (change the tempo and style of the music)
- in the school cafeteria during lunch preparation

Found in Nature

Nature provides a source for many writing activities. As your students look at poems by famous poets, they will find that nature provides a frequently-used theme. It's an easy topic because it is readily available to all writers and has so many variations. By exploring nature in pre-writing exercises, students will have a backlog of ideas for poems that deal with nature. When they actually write their poems they can use these ideas to describe the colors, smells, or sights of nature, or, like many writers, they can use nature for a metaphor for other seemingly-unrelated things.

The following suggestions are nature writing ideas that can be used for daily journaling, brainstorming, listing, or writing poetry and stories.

1. Use the following topics for brainstorming about nature. Instruct students to write all of the words or phrases they can think of about a topic in a timed period (anywhere from one to five minutes). Keep adding to this list.

flowers	snakes
birds	lizards
insects	ice
ponds	snow
lakes	rain
rivers	rabbits
streams	sun
wind	lightning
balmy breezes	sand
flies	water
bees	swamps
dragonflies	frogs
butterflies	crickets
grass	humidity
weeds	leaves
puddles	fish
trees	alligators
squirrels	cattails
worms	roses

2. Ask students to think creatively by making creative comparisons about things. Ask them to name several reasons the following things are similar.

How are streams like life?
How is the wind like anger?
How are dragonflies like paper?
How are crickets like money?
How is a snake like a television?
How are trees like stars in the night sky?
How are weeds like pudding?
How is humidity like a Cadillac?
How are worms like cities?
How is the grass like the flu?
How are puddles like pennies?
How is snow like a kite?
How are leaves like vacations?
How are squirrels like beach balls?
How is ice like an airplane?
How are balmy breezes like jeans?
How are frogs like tennis racquets?
How is the sun like a fence post?
How are rabbits like paper plates?
How are bees like violins?
How is lightning like a shovel?

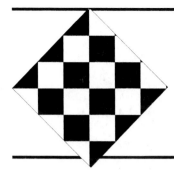

Chapter 3

Entrées

Ideas for unique poetry writing

How do you motivate students to write creatively? One way is to give them creative assignments. The assignments in this section provide delectable choices of lessons for writing original poetry. Using themes that are appealing to students, the exercises in this section offer a diverse array of starters for writing poetry. This wonderful, all-you-can-eat buffet offers many taste temptations. Enjoy the sizzling goodness of humorous verses, nature-oriented rhyme schemes, nonsensical prose, and an abundant supply of different opportunities to write poetry.

Lemonade

■ Overview

Students reflect on life's experiences and create poetry about a single event that caused some bad memories but through which they were able to manage some positive results.

■ Objectives

- Students will list events from their lives that have caused mixed emotions.
- Students will demonstrate their ability to write story poems about one of life's memorable events.
- Students will demonstrate the ability to recognize that good things can come from bad by alternating the two occurrences within their poems.

■ Materials

✓ paper
✓ pens or pencils
✓ copies of pages 25 and 26

■ Procedure

1. Begin the lesson by writing the following statement on the board: "When life gives you lemons, make lemonade." The discussion of this quote should focus on the fact that life's happenings can produce a variety of emotions, some of which are very conflicting. The students are to think about events that can be bad in many ways, but at the same time they can also provide some good memories. This is often a difficult concept for students to grasp, so it is strongly recommended that some of the following examples be given.
   - Middle school years (best of times) - growing up, more privileges, dances, boyfriend/girlfriends
     Middle school years (worst of times) - relationship with parents is changing, friendships are changing, more responsibilities, more homework
   - Birthday party (best of times) - great presents, lots of fun, wonderful food
     Birthday party (worst of times) - getting into a fight with a best friend, a new camera or CD is broken
   - Christmas holidays (best of times) - surrounded by a family's love, receiving a special gift, wonderful food, snow
     Christmas holidays (worst of times) - car accident on the trip home, a bad cold, bad weather

2. Involve students in a pre-writing brainstorming session in which they are to list single events from their lives that have created both good and bad memories.

■ Poem Format

The poem will consist of eight to twelve verses, alternating between a worst case scenario and a best case scenario for the same event. Students should begin the poem with the line, "It was the best and the worst of ____" (the subject of the poem will go in place of the line).

The next line should be a worst happening, followed by a best happening, and so on. After each line write a word or a phrase that best exemplifies the mood or the emotion felt at that time. See the examples on page 25.

■ Option

The poem can be written in two separate sections, one about the best of times and the other about the worst of times.

■ Evaluation

- Use of conflicting thoughts, feelings, and emotions
- Class participation and discussion
- Completion of a poem that follows the prescribed format

Christmas Vacation

It was the best and worst of vacations...
   Florida.
Frozen, icy highways, the smell of something burning under the hood,
   Panic!
Sandy beaches, balmy breezes, sun-filled day,
   Paradise!
Searching endlessly for an able mechanic on Christmas Eve,
   Hopeless!
A tropical rainstorm and the sparkling turquoise water,
   Surreal!
A sudden "crash;" the sirens of approaching emergency vehicles,
   Pain!
Looking out on the Gulf at a rainbow-colored sun setting on the water,
   Breathtaking!
Madly rushing to catch a flight in a damaged vehicle; missing the plane!
   Despair!
Lying on the beach, a picnic with seagulls, and seafood at a dockside restaurant,
   Delicious!
Tears, a two-hour delay, and a side-tracked flight to Miami,
   Exhaustion!
Finally, Christmas Eve with loved ones; strains of "Silent Night" mixing
   with sounds of the surf pounding the shore...
   Peace!
It was the best of vacations; it was the worst of vacations.

The Motorcycle Ride

It was the best and worst of rides.
A motorcycle.
The engine roared,
   Terror.
My heart raced,
   Titillation.
The sensation of being off balance,
   Insecurity.
The wind whipping against my face,
   Independence.
I think I might die,
I feel like I can fly,
It was the worst ride; it was the best ride.

Seeing the Good and Bad Sides of Something

Directions

Lemonade poetry is poetry that tells about events or situations that consist of conflicting feelings. These could be situations that had both a mix of good and bad experiences and therefore produced conflicting feelings. They could also be situations where you took a difficult experience and turned it into something pleasant.

Remember events from the past that created memories that were both unpleasant and wonderful all at the same time. List them on a sheet of paper. From your list, select the one memory that has given you the most remarkable conflicts and write a story poem following the format below.

- **First line** - Begin with the words, "It was the best and the worst of ___."

- **Second line** - One word that names the subject of the poem (for example, vacations, birthdays, holidays, or school years).

- **Third line** - A poetic phrase that describes one of the *bad* things that happened during this time period.

- **Fourth line** - One word or a short phrase that best sums up the event or your feelings about it in the preceding line.

- **Fifth line** - A poetic phrase that describes one of the *good* things that happened during this time period.

- **Sixth line** - A single word or a short phrase that sums up the good event or your feelings about it.

- **Following Lines** - Alternate the next several lines, using a bad and a good happening, followed by a single descriptive emotion-packed word each time. There should be a total of four or five good and bad memories in all.

- **Last Line** - The last line of the poem should say; "It was the worst of _____. It was the best of _____."

Show Me

Overview

By stretching their creative thinking abilities, students transform basic, no-frills sentences into descriptive poetry that paints pictures using words.

Objectives

- Students will generate lists of words and phrases that are descriptive of a given topic.
- Students will demonstrate the ability to turn basic sentences into descriptive poems that use alternative phrasing and words in place of the existing sentence.

Materials

✓ copies of pages 28 and 29
✓ paper
✓ pens or pencils

Procedure

1. This lesson on descriptive poetry should begin with a group collaboration poem. Write a basic sentence on the board, such as "The pizza was good." Ask students to respond to the following questions:
   - Does this sentence adequately describe how good the pizza was?
   - Did you get a mental picture of the pizza?
   - What words or phrases might be used to show how the pizza tasted instead of using the word "good?"

2. Ask students to think of many alternatives to the meaning of "good." As students generate alternative words and phrasings for "The pizza was good," write them in paragraph form on the board as they are suggested.

3. Read these responses aloud and ask the class if they can now get a more descriptive picture of how the pizza tasted, looked, smelled, felt, or possibly sounded.

4. Ask the class to pull out the important phrases and put them into a poetic format. They should not use the same descriptive word in the "Show-Me" poem that is used in the simple topic sentence. For example, the word "good" should not be used at all during the descriptive writing of the poem.

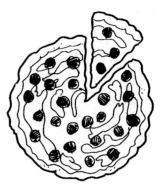

Sample Poem

Delightful, enticing aroma,
Oozing with hot, juicy cheeses,
And bubbling tomato sauce.
It boasts a variety of exotic spices,
Nestled comfortably in a thick buttery crust.
One bite takes you to paradise.

5. Students are to select a topic sentence from the list on page 29.

6. Allow time for each student to brainstorm a list of words or phrases that would better describe the topic sentence. Instruct them to pull out the most important and descriptive components and write them in poetic form.

Students should be instructed not to just list synonyms for the words in the sentences. Instead, they should be encouraged to incorporate comparisons (such as similes and metaphors) in order to produce more successful descriptive writing.

Evaluation

- Ability to paint pictures with words
- Poem that shows creativity and originality
- Use of comparisons throughout the poem

The teacher was angry

As she stood in front of the classroom,
We knew we were in trouble.
Smoke poured from her ears and her nose,
Making her look like a fire-eating dragon.
Her hands trembled as she hurled
    post-it-notes and paperclips.
She picked up unsuspecting students
One by the hair on his head,
Another by his ears,
Causing both to scream in pain!
Suddenly she bellowed,
"Why did you not do your homework?"
                    by Jason J.

The dancer had good rhythm

Rat-a-tat, rat-a-tat.
The enunciated sounds bounce off the floor.
In perfect syncopation, they resound,
Solid sounds,
Spellbinding sounds.
Rat-a-tat, tat, tat.
The dancer composes a symphony of beats,
A blithe pattern of accents and pauses.
The right foot mimics the music,
The left foot answers.
Rat-a-tat, rat-a-tat, rat-a-tat, tat, tat.
A rising wave of perfectly placed steps,
A silent turn on tip toes,
Tah-tah, it ends.

He is handsome

The air was cold and icy,
It whipped the trees in circles,
And sent all inside,
To be by their hearths.
One lone youth stood on the veranda,
His strong hands gripped the banister,
And calm, blue eyes searched the horizon.
Boyish lips smiled,
As he realized he was alone.
He ran his fingers through his hair,
Dark locks that framed his face,
And he heaved a sigh,
Deep enough to match the winds.
He liked being lonely;
He liked the cold.
They would never understand him
These people inside,
Hiding from the world.
But the beauty of his face,
Did neither mar nor take away from
The depth and understanding
That lived in his heart.
He clenched his strong jaw,
And turned to face the cold.
His brow furrowed in concentration
As he watched the stars begin to fade.
His face belonged among those
shining in the night.
So is the young and valiant prince
Searching for eternal youth and life?
He shed a tear,
But did not know why.
It dropped below,
To aid the living ground
And left a reminding mark upon his cheek.
                    by Martha Gary

Show Me with Words

With this poetry assignment you will be using descriptive language to paint a picture for the reader. Choose a common phrase and write words and phrases that will describe in detail what this sentence could mean. Combine the phrases into a poem. Try use rhythm, repetition or rhyme to give your descriptions some consistency.

The couch was comfortable.

The crowd was large.

The boy/girl had an attitude.

The light was dim.

The shoes were too tight.

The garbage smelled bad.

The dress was pretty.

She had a headache.

The homework was difficult.

The man was strong.

The day was hot.

The dancer had good rhythm.

The lights were colorful.

The bed was comfortable.

The room was a mess.

The movie was funny.

The horn was loud.

Everyone was laughing.

The picnic was fun.

The light was bright.

The pizza was good.

The ceilings are high.

The snowfall was beautiful.

The school cafeteria was noisy.

The amusement park was busy.

The snow was bright.

The man's hair was dirty.

The roller coaster was scary.

The song was sad.

The day was cold.

The storm was scary.

My mother/father was mad.

The baby was cute.

The girl was beautiful.

The class was boring.

The vacation was fun.

The fire was warm.

The band was loud.

The monkey was funny.

The mountains were large.

The dog was playful.

The house was run down.

The day was rainy.

He was handsome.

The table was filled with food.

The hamburger smelled wonderful.

The child was naughty.

The ocean was calm.

The cookies were good.

The car went fast.

The dog had bad breath.

The sunset had many colors.

The ants ruined the picnic.

The grass needed mowing.

Exposing Prejudice

Overview

Students read, brainstorm and reflect upon various types of prejudice that exist in the world today, and they write poetry concerning these issues.

Objectives

- Students will read a variety of short stories, poems and books that involve some form of prejudice.
- Students will brainstorm different types of prejudice.
- Students will rank their own personal lists of prejudicial problems on a scale of 1 to 10 (10 being an issue that causes the highest degree of stress).
- Students will write pattern poems about four different kinds of prejudice.
- Students will demonstrate an ability to write reflectively about important prejudicial issues.

Materials

✓ paper
✓ pens or pencils
✓ chalkboard or large sheet of bulletin board paper to be used for brainstorming
✓ copies of page 32

Procedure

1. **Pre-Lesson**

   You have two options for teaching students about prejudice:

   Option 1: The study of prejudice may be taught as a single, isolated lesson culminating in the poetry assignment.

   Option 2: Prejudice may be taught as an in-depth literature unit based on several books and short stories.

In either case, the procedures for the poetry assignment will be the same.

Ask students to list different types of prejudice. The examples should be written on a chalkboard or a large sheet of bulletin board paper. Some examples are: intellectual prejudice, racial prejudice, social prejudice, financial prejudice, religious prejudice, regional prejudice, age prejudice, physical prejudice, fashion sense prejudice, weight prejudice, speech prejudice, or gender prejudice.

2. Select a couple of short stories and at least one novel to study. If option 2 is used, the following books or short stories are highly recommended for use in the literature study:

   - Short stories: *Harrison Bergeron,* by Kurt Vonnegut (futuristic story that attempts to eliminate all prejudice); *Seventh Grade,* by Lynda Barry (racial and social prejudice); and *Flowers For Algernon* by Daniel Keyes (intellectual prejudice).

   - Books/novels: *Night* by Elie Wiesel (religious and racial prejudice); *The Outsiders* by S.E. Hinton (social prejudice); and *The Pearl* by John Steinbeck (social/financial prejudice).

3. **The Poetry Assignment**

   The prejudice poem consists of six, four-line verses in the student's choice of a rhymed or non-rhymed format.

   - The **first verse** consists of each student's own definition of prejudice.

   - The **next four verses** each depict a different type of prejudice.

   - The **last verse** is an offering of the student's solution or resolution to the problem of prejudice.

   A reproducible handout with the format for the poem can be found on page 32.

   The poem can be written from many different viewpoints. Students may choose to write about incidents they have experienced in their lives or in the lives of others. They may decide to write from a generic point of view, based on their knowledge of the world (not from direct experiences).

4. Some of the following questions should be considered by students when they are writing the final verse of this poem:

   - Is it possible for us to be equal in every way?

   - If not, what can we do to make people kinder and more loving toward one another?

   - What have I personally done to effect change regarding the issue of prejudice?

   - How was I personally affected when some form of prejudice was directed at me?

■ **Variation**

Although the goal of this assignment is to teach students that prejudice exists in many forms, teachers may choose to assign only one issue of prejudice rather than four different types.

■ **Evaluation**

- Understanding of the diversity of prejudice.

- A poem about an important issue.

- Knowledge of literature through participation in class discussions.

- Knowledge of self by ranking a list of prejudicial issues.

■ **Extensions**

- Write a short story about a prejudicial issue.

- Using the Future Problem Solving method, create a list of solutions for solving the problem of prejudice in the world.

Prejudice Examined

Why is the world against me for what I am?
A small minority in majority's land.
Just 'cause we're we, they won't lend us a hand;
Superiority's the authority, but I do what I can.
"Little sun chile, why you so black?"
"Why you so light?" another child retorts back.
"Your kind gets all the breaks," my daddy say.
"Why child, you, were you born this way?"
Popularity standards frown on excess pounds,
Yet on anorexic issues they'll also hound.
So weight is also now a burden on our chests,
For we rather, lithe and lissome (Ogden Nash said it best).
If a woman rises above her "station,"
Then, it's her "curves" that won her "that situation."
But if one receives recognition for a single sincere stand,
Then we say, "Oh well, it's just the man."
The obscenely rich will get their due someday,
While the poor are still yet turned away.
They don't stand a chance improving their circumstances,
Their families they can't feed, 'cause they don't have the finances.
Now to those who by prejudice choose to daily live,
I do offer this dismissal:
That we all fluctuate and learn to freely give,
Love the man for what's inside, and forget the superficial.
                    by Jennifer Cornelius

Directions

Think carefully about all of the different types of prejudice that exist in the world today and write your poem based on your feelings about these issues. The poem may be rhymed or unrhymed, but you must use the correct number of lines and verses, as suggested below.

Verse 1 - Lines 1-4   Define prejudice in your own words.
Verse 2 - Lines 5-8   Discuss one type of prejudice.
Verse 3 - Lines 9-12   Discuss another type of prejudice.
Verse 4 - Lines 13-16   Discuss a different type of prejudice.
Verse 5 - Lines 17-20   Discuss a fourth type of prejudice.
Verse 6 - Lines 21-24   Discuss your solutions to the problems of prejudice.

Star Poetry

Overview

Students select one of life's issues and expand their thinking to debate five points (as in a star) either for or against this issue.

Objectives

- Students will determine which side of the selected issue they wish to represent.
- Students will locate and list all possible information concerning the side of the issue they have chosen to represent.
- The student will write five-point star poems.

Materials

✓ paper
✓ pens or pencils
✓ copies of pages 34 and 35
✓ reference materials

Procedure

1. Give out copies of page 34. Read through the life issues and allow students to select topics. If you wish, you can add topics that are relevant to your community or student body.

2. Have students brainstorm (pre-write) their initial feelings about the topic, based on any knowledge they already have about the subject. After doing this, they should commit to a side of the issue — for or against.

    Note: You may wish to assign a side for each student to take.

3. Students should locate any information they can find about their subject and make a list of all the points that best reflect their stand. They are to list all of their points and categorize them into five general areas on a star pattern as shown on the bottom of page 35.

4. Students should then pick out the five best arguments and write a four-line verse with an A-B-C-B pattern for each argument. When completed, all five poetry points will be written in the form of a continuous poem that lists each separate point.

Pattern

The pattern is :
   Title - Name of the issue selected
   Point 1
   These four lines cover the first point of the selected issue.
   line 1 - A
   line 2 - B
   line 3 - C
   line 4 - B (rhymes with line 2)
   Point 2
   Follow the same pattern as in point 1. Repeat for points 3, 4, and 5.

Note

There is no set pattern for how students write each verse. The only constant is the rhyming pattern. They may introduce each point in whatever creative way they wish. See the example.

Evaluation

- Poem that is well thought out and follows the correct rhyming scheme
- Knowledge of the subject matter
- The five points are well made

Extensions

- Ask the students to defend the stands they took on the issues in formal debates.
- Students can write letters to the editor of their local newspapers about their concerns about these issues.

The issue: **Teenage Smoking**
Side taken: against

Point 1: Standing on a street corner,
Looking, oh so tough.
People passing by,
Thinking you are rough.

Point 2: The fumes are all around you,
Fouling up the air.
Causing you to cough and sputter,
And stinking up your hair.

Point 3: Your lungs are getting blacker,
They're filled with soot and grime.
You're going to get sicker,
If you keep smoking all the time.

Point 4: Going into stores,
Pretending that you're older.
Breaking laws this young,
Can make you even bolder.

Point 5: If you start smoking young,
You may think you're cool.
But you can become addicted,
And then you're just a fool.

Healthy Living

Eat some fresh-picked peas,
Some wholesome carrots too,
Get your fill of healthy foods,
It's the smartest thing to do.

Get off the couch and exercise,
Walk, jog, swim and run.
Soon you'll come to realize,
That exercise is fun.

Keep stress in tow,
Slow down your pace,
Take a long, deep breath,
The stress-free life embrace.

Always wear your seat belt,
Drive with caution and with care,
Deal patiently with traffic jams,
Stay alert and stay aware.

Look for the bright side,
Take a positive stance.
Balance work with play time,
And your health you will enhance.

Life's Issues — Pro or Con?

divorce	popularity	parental control of:
driving age	dating age	◆ clothes
curfews	censorship of music	◆ hair/makeup
grades	homework	◆ extracurricular activities
year-long school	school dress codes	◆ television viewing
smoking	video games	◆ friends
computer blocking	animal rights	
drugs or alcohol	tattooing or piercing	
movie ratings		

Directions

Make a star. Write each one of your five arguments in each of the five points of the star. Use the area around the star to write ideas related to each point. After you have organized your thoughts, combine them into a five-verse poem.

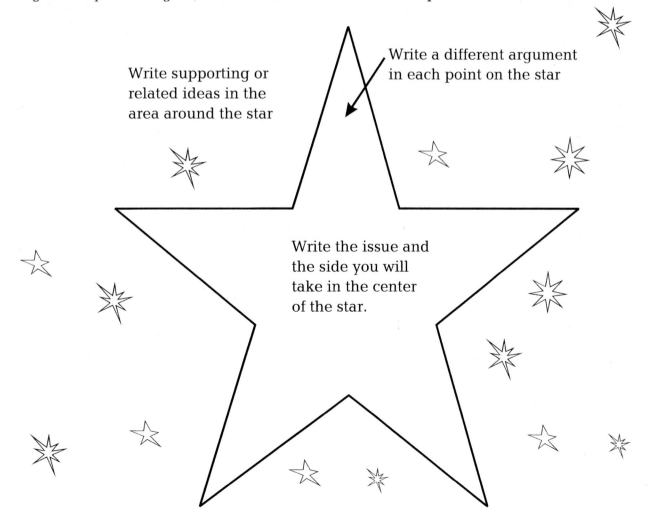

Write supporting or related ideas in the area around the star

Write a different argument in each point on the star

Write the issue and the side you will take in the center of the star.

Changing Beliefs

◼ Overview

The students are asked to write poetry based on fictional or real childhood beliefs that are subject to change over the course of several years.

◼ Objectives

- Students will write poems, rhymed or un-rhymed, consisting of four to eight verses that reflect inconsistencies in childhood and adolescent beliefs.
- Students will demonstrate knowledge of either their own belief system or that of others in their own age group.
- Students will effectively summarize the whole concept of the poem in the last verse.
- Students will design a creative border to go around the poem.

◼ Materials

✓ paper
✓ pens and pencils
✓ copies of page 37

◼ Procedure

1. As a pre-writing activity, ask students to make a list of all the things they believed in as young children but no longer feel are true. Some examples that might be discussed and written on the board are: Santa Claus, the Easter Bunny, the Tooth Fairy, the belief that their parents are very rich, etc. Next, they are to continue adding to these lists, this time naming beliefs that others in their age group might have had over the years.

2. Students have a choice of two different types of poems: a poem that reflects the student's own childhood beliefs (this can be very humorous), or a poem that reflects the beliefs of others in their age group, but does not necessarily reflect their own personal views. They should review their lists and choose one of these formats.

3. Each poem will consist of three to eight verses of four lines each (see reproducible on page 37). Each line is to begin with the words "I used to believe…", and the second line is to begin with the words "But now I…" The last two lines of each verse explain the second line. Students should elaborate on whether they hold the same beliefs at this time. This repetition continues until the very last verse, where each student is to summarize his/her feelings about the whole theme of the poem. This last verse has no set pattern and can be as many as five lines.

4. When finished, students may create attractive borders to go around the edges of the poem.

◼ Evaluation

- Poetry that shows old beliefs compared to new beliefs
- Knowledge of his or her own belief system
- Well-constructed poem
- A summary in the last verse that pulls together the final thoughts about the theme

◼ Extensions

- Students can turn their poems into songs and perform them for the class.
- One of the beliefs written about in one of the verses can be turned into a short story.

❖ *Beliefs* **Sample Poetry**

I Used to Believe

I used to believe that night was scary,
But now I'm calm at twilight.
Feeling the quiet, basking in the silence,
Letting the day's turmoil give way to peace.

I used to believe that I could sing like a bird,
But now I can dance like a bee.
Moving with speed and grace,
I have discovered my true talent.

I used to believe that dogs were boys and cats were girls,
But now I have my genders straight.
Whether they bark, meow, bleat, twitter, or moo,
All animals have boy offspring and little girls too.

I used to believe everything I was told,
Imagined things transformed themselves into realities.
Unsure and naive I grasped at unlikely explanations.
Now I question, I explore, I examine.
Old beliefs give way to new realities.

Directions

This poetry assignment is all about things that you believed when you were much younger. These same beliefs have changed as you have gotten older. Make a list of things that you once believed in. Now take several of these beliefs and write a poem about them.

The format of each verse, with the exception of the last verse, should be as follows.

- ✓ Line 1   Begins with the words "I used to believe"
  (*write a belief you used to hold*)
- ✓ Line 2   "But now I..." (*write your current beliefs*)
- ✓ Lines 3 and 4   These two lines should explain why this belief no longer exists.
- ✓ There should be at least three to eight verses that follow this same pattern, each one about a different belief.
- ✓ In the last verse summarize your feelings about the poem's theme.

© *Poetry à la Carte* • Prufrock Press Inc**37**

Home Town

Overview

Students are asked to research, explore and write poetry about their home town or city.

Objectives

- Students will locate information about their home town's history.
- Students will describe the "essence" of their home town.
- Students will write descriptive poems about their towns.
- Students will photograph or sketch scenes that show the essence of their city or town.

Materials

✓ copies of page 39
✓ paper
✓ sketch pads/cameras
✓ reference materials
✓ pens or pencils
✓ a computer

Procedure

1. Start several days or weeks before the poetry lesson by having students brainstorm a list of descriptive words or phrases about their city.

2. The students will then begin gathering materials and information about the city in which they live. They are to locate and write facts about each of the following:
    - population, geographical location, and physical size
    - the early history and settlement
    - tourist attractions
    - historical sites
    - famous people and events
    - any war associations

3. Taking all of the information gathered, along with their list of words, students will write poems about the city. They are to use one of the three topics below. Whatever topic they choose, they need to understand that they must communicate the essence of the town and show their home town in a positive light. The three formats from which to choose are:

    ★ **Places that make our city unique**
    Students name four places that make their home town special and then use descriptive words or phrases that reflect why these places make this city wonderful.

    ★ **Why the city is beautiful**
    Students select four things that make their town or city beautiful and list words or phrases about each thing that reflect this beauty.

    ★ **The four seasons of my town**
    Incorporate words or phrases that show how this particular city is special during each season.

4. Ask students to sketch or photograph an interesting site that best shows "the essence" described in their poetry.

Evaluation

- The descriptive nature of the poem
- The quality of the sketch or photograph
- The essence of the city presented in the poetry

Extensions

- Take students on a photographic or sketching field trip to the downtown area of your town.

Four Seasons of Jackson

Sunny,
Bright,
Hot and humid,
Those are Jackson summers!

Colorful,
Warm,
A breeze in the air,
Jackson autumns are very
beautiful!

Cold,
Foggy,
Piercing winds,
Jackson winters are always a
wonder.

Balmy,
Windy,
Fresh and happy,
Jackson springs are the best
time of year.
by Nailah Horne

Old Mission Town

The mission is your nucleus.
Ancient, staunch, a relic of bygone days,
It is still the heart of the city, the center of
    activity.

The river wanders aimlessly through your core,
Once a source of livelihood,
Now the fountain of tranquility and tourism,
It flows with reserve in a sea of activity.

Green hills cradle you,
Tumbling humpity-dumpity from summit to sea,
Defining your borders, inviting hikers,
Framing both sunrise and sunset.

From the dust of the past,
Into the hubbub of the present,
You have survived,
You are alive,
You are my favorite old mission town.

Directions

 Choose one of these three formats for your poem:
  ✷ Places that make our city unique
  ✷ Why the city is beautiful
  ✷ The four seasons of my town

 Write a poem that presents the "essence" of your town.

 Your poem should be at least three stanzas long and should use descriptive words
    that paint a picture for the reader. You may wish to follow this format:
  ✷ line 1 - name of the object, place or season
  ✷ lines 2 - 3 - descriptive words and phrases about line 1
  ✷ line 4 - a sentence that sums up the thoughts in this stanza.

Poetry by the Numbers

◆ Overview

Students reflect on childhood memories or special people and write poetry using a syllabic format.

◆ Objectives

- Students will list memories or attributes of people who are special to them.
- Students will demonstrate the ability to count and use syllables in poetry.
- Students will develop poems about their memories and write them in the correct syllabication format.

◆ Materials

✓ pens and pencils
✓ paper
✓ copies of pages 41 and 42

◆ Procedure

1. Give students five minutes to list memorable events from the past or to select people who are special to them and note characteristics of these people. The memories can be things they always think about when asked about their childhood. Examples might be a favorite birthday party or present, a holiday vacation, the first time they got up on water skis, or an award or honor they received. If writing about a special person, they may want to consider several people as subjects of their poems. They can then select one person and write a list of attributes for this person. After they have brainstormed for the five-minute period, they should be able to narrow their subjects down to one or two memories or two or three special features of the person.

2. Once they have narrowed their choices down to one or two, they are ready to complete the questionnaire on page 42. After filling out this sheet they are to write the number pattern obtained by answering the ten questions. This will become the format of their poem. There will be ten lines in the poem, and each of these lines will consist of the number of syllables derived from the worksheet.

The poem should be unrhymed and will consist of ten lines in all. Each student will have a different format, based on the digits from their lives. When students come up with zeros, they should use the number 10 for the number of digits.

◆ Evaluation

- Ability to write sensible lines consisting of a certain number of syllables
- A meaningful poem about a childhood memory or about a special person

◆ Extensions

- This is a good lead in for writing Haiku poetry.

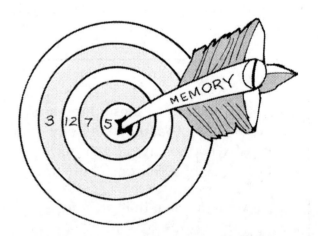

Laurie

My oldest child with eyes of blue,
Shiny brown hair,
And loving,
She strives for perfection.
Her abilities are endless.
Stubborn,
With a voice like an angel,
Her creativity knows no bounds,
Laurie Elizabeth,
The daughter of my dreams!

Samantha

Samantha is a blonde-haired child,
With eyes of blue,
That sparkle.
Sam, free as Brother Wind…
Her spirit is willful and fun!
Lovely,
My youngest child, Samantha.
She brightens up the world around her,
And leaves an afterglow
Long after she's gone.

Ski Trip

Skiing in Colorado,
Breckenridge.
Fun at the lodge,
And snow falling in a heavy storm.
Flying down the icy slopes,
On a freezing cold, winter's morn,
Hot chocolate by the fire.
We're worn out and sleepy,
Ready for a new day
Of fun, sun, snow, and play.

Your Poetic Numbers

Answer each of the following questions and write the answers to each question on the blanks that follow the questions. These ten numbers (in order) will become the number of syllables in each line of a poem. The poem will be unrhymed.

a. Your age minus 3 _____

b. The number of letters in your first name (not your nickname,
   but your real first name) _____

c. The number of people in your family (include siblings, stepparents,
   and half-brothers and sisters) _____

d. The number of letters in your last name_____

e. The number of letters in your city or town _____

f. The last number in your telephone number _____

g. The third number in your social security number _____

h. The last number in your year of birth _____

i. The first number in your zip code _____

j. The number of your aunts, uncles and first cousins,
   minus 3 _____

Write the numbers you will use in your poem here.

a._____ b._____ c._____ d._____ e._____ f._____ g._____ h._____ i._____ j._____

Nonsense Poems

Overview

Students will create nonsensical, fun, and meaningless poetry to be read aloud. This format is especially appealing for those students who are unmotivated by more serious formats.

Objectives

- Students will write poems about subjects that are nonsensical.
- Students will demonstrate their abilities to use rhyme.
- Students will read their poems aloud in class.

Materials

✓ copies of page 44
✓ paper
✓ pens and pencils
✓ If needed, the list of "Totally Ridiculous Things to Write About" sheet (page 45)

Procedure

1. If you have not already presented information on personification, rhyme and repetition, do so at this time. For a good example of the use of rhyme and repetition in a poem, read Edgar Allan Poe's "The Bells."

2. Select one of the following options:
   - **Option 1**
     Students choose a common article that is not very poetic by nature. Examples might be chairs, coats, silly string, the school bus, pencils, the dictionary, shoes or bones. They write about the subject as if it had human characteristics (personification). The poem should be at least three verses (four lines each) with consistent repetition and/or rhyming scheme.

   - **Option 2**
     Students are to select one word from each column on the "Totally Ridiculous Things to Write About" sheet found on page 45. Once they have chosen three words, they are to connect them in poems of three to four verses that rhyme. The poems can be funny and ridiculous and do not have to make sense.

Evaluation

- The ability to connect unusual combinations of words in a poem.
- Use of rhyme.
- Oral presentation of poem, read with expression and enthusiasm.

Extensions

- Students can write stories such as "How the _____ Got Its Name," using the three unrelated words.
- Students can illustrate their nonsensical poems.

■ Option 1

Directions

Pick a frivolous topic or a simple, commonplace object. Examples might be rats, garbage, macaroni and cheese, or chairs. Then write a poem about the topic. Repeat the name of the object several times for emphasis.

■ Option 2

Directions

Select one word from each column on the page titled "Totally Ridiculous Things to Write About." Connect these words and create a nonsensical, rhyming poem about the three words. The following poem used the words: shrinking, pencils, snowboarding.

Sample Poems

Chairs!

Just sitting there during all kinds of
    weather,
Waiting for something to happen.
Chairs!
Some are fuzzy,
Some are plastic,
Some are made of leather.
Chairs!
Some chairs are built low to the ground.
Chairs!
Some are soft and some are hard,
And some are big and round.
Chairs!
Chairs are friends in our time of need,
Offering us a great place to rest and
    read.
We love you, chairs!

Shrinking Pencils Snowboarding

The shrinking pencils of Colorado,
Were in a hurry and a great big rush,
To snowboard the slopes before there was slush.

They loaded their gear and rode the ski lift,
To get to the top before the end of the day,
To "sharpen" their skills before the last sun's ray.

They got shorter as the daylight waned,
Lying on snowboards with their pencil thin backs,
Erasing behind them any signs of their tracks.

When they got to the bottom of the skiing slope,
They were tired and eager for a nice warm bed,
And a sharpened point with plenty of lead.

But, alas those poor pencils couldn't go any further,
And no one nearby could hear their call,
So they made their last mark in that ski lodge hall.

Totally Ridiculous Things to Write About

Select one word from each column and use these words as a topic for a poem.

Column A	Column B	Column C
stuck-up	windows	scaring
sluggish	lizards	doodling
mean	cheese	surfing
prehistoric	teddy bears	shrinking
leathery	wallpaper	dancing
ornery	parachutes	warping
supercilious	mattresses	applauding
talkative	crayons	loitering
evil	sea bass	reading
shrinking	pizzas	sighing
super	posters	drowning
favorite	pupils	ringing
spidery	pencils	singing
entertaining	backpacks	laughing
drooping	chairs	hiding
drenched	goats	lying
languid	pickles	kicking
kooky	computers	jumping
nosy	violets	parking
resistant	notebooks	wiggling
total	trains	hurting
whimpering	ears	eating
wily	candles	typing
compatible	couches	burning
blistered	wood chips	building
athletic	rockets	snowboarding
irritating	VCRs	swimming
regrettable	cameras	sliding
wrongful	handles	raining
yucky	refrigerators	riding
sloppy	toes	comparing
favorite	soldiers	bungee-jumping

Treasure Hunt

This poetry assignment is a lot of fun, but it requires thoughtful preparation by the teacher. Students work in groups to write collaborative poetry that will lead other groups of students to find treasure either within the classroom or outside on the school campus.

■ Overview

Students are asked to work collaboratively in groups of four or five to write poetry that leads others to find treasure.

■ Objectives

- Students will demonstrate the ability to work well with a group.
- Students will design unique, creative clues for the treasure hunters.
- Students will write poems in four-line verses that rhyme.
- Students will locate treasure by following clues written by members of other groups.

■ Materials

✓ copies of page 47
✓ paper
✓ pens and pencils
✓ treasure items - These items should be printed out on pieces of paper and then glued to gold, foil-wrapped money candy or bright yellow construction paper pieces. Pictures of each treasure item are included on page 48.

■ Procedure

1. Divide the class into groups of four or five students, and give each group a set of the pictured treasure items.

2. Instruct students to make a list of places where they will hide the clues. It is important that they do this first, so that they will have a plan of what they're going to write about. If possible, try to have two indoor locations and two outdoor locations.

Option:
You may ask the groups to draw a treasure map, showing all the locations for buried treasure.

3. Students should then write rhymed, four-line poems for each picture on page 48. The format of each poetic clue should be four lines long and it must rhyme in some way. It is important that students write their poetry clues with some attempt to make them difficult, but not impossible to find. The teacher should approve all of the clues before allowing the students to hide them.

4. After the clue poems have been written, the students will go by teams and hide the clues in the proper places, saving the first clue to give to the team that will be searching for their buried treasure. Teachers should have previously determined which teams will be matched up to hunt for clues.

Give all of the teams a time limit that is adequate to search for the treasure. When one of the teams turns in all 16 of their treasure items, they are the winners of the hunt.

■ Evaluation

- Clues that lead to specific locations
- Use of a four-line rhyming pattern for the clues

The following "Treasure Hunt" poem is a sampling of clues written by student teams in an eighth grade class.

You're going to find diamonds
In a most unusual place,
Look hard in the room
In a very cluttered place.

Behind the bookcase
What a treasure you'll see,
A beautiful automobile
Don't you wish there were three?

If you'd like a nice party
You'll need a great cake,
Look near the door
Close to something that's fake.

A fantastic new cell phone
Is waiting for you,
It's very, very close
To where you found clue number two.

If you want to be royalty
Then you'll need a good crown,
It's under the papers we wrote
About our home town.

Oh how wonderful
To own a new sailboat,
Just look all around
And find it under a coat.

Look at the bulletin board
And study it well,
You'll find bags of money
But where? We won't tell.

A boom box is wonderful
When you're marooned on the beach,
It's close to your teacher,
But it's out of your reach!

Directions

For this project you will work in a team. These are the steps you will follow:

- Your team will receive 16 pieces of paper that represent 16 different treasures.

- Decide where you will hide each treasure.

- Write clues that will direct other people to the locations where the treasures are hidden.

- Each clue should be four lines and should rhyme.

- Save the first clue but hide the other clues in such a way that the location for the first object will also have the second clue, the location for the second item will have the third clue, and so forth.

Cut out the pictures and glue or tape them to gold foil-wrapped candy money or construction paper.

Write a poetic clue for each one of these treasures.

Ode to a Hero

■ Overview

After careful discussion and reflection, students are asked to write poetry about their real-life heroes.

■ Objectives

- Students will write definitions of a hero.
- Students will list heroes from history, contemporary heroes, and unsung heroes.
- Students will develop criteria for what makes a hero.
- Students will create poems about their or own real-life hero.

■ Materials

- ✓ paper
- ✓ pens or pencils
- ✓ chalkboard or large sheets of bulletin board paper
- ✓ copies of pages 50 and 51

■ Procedure

1. Prior to any discussion, ask students to individually write definitions of a hero. Share these definitions and make a list of ideas. Discuss the merits of each criterion. Have students go back and revise their original definitions, if necessary.

2. The next step is to have students reflect on heroes from the past and present to better understand the true meaning of the word "hero." Have students fill in the "Heroes" worksheet (page 51). Ask them why these people were special. How did they stand out from other people? Discuss unsung heroes. These are people who serve as positive role models. Some examples might be parents, siblings, other relatives, youth directors, teachers, friends, religious leaders.

3. After completing this worksheet, each child should select one person from his or her list of unsung heroes who has been a personal real-life hero to him or her. Each student should write some reasons why this person is a hero.

4. Students are to write poems dedicated to their real-life heroes. The poem may be rhymed or unrhymed. Each student should first decide whether the hero should be named at the beginning of the poem or revealed at the end of the poem.

   Samples:
   The poem may resemble, but is not limited to, one of the following two forms:

   - **Option1**
     The first option is to provide several reasons why that person is a hero and back it up by citing several examples.

   - **Option 2**
     The second option of is one in which the hero is metaphorically compared to a variety of objects. Students should use at least six metaphors in their poems.

■ Evaluation

- Completion of the worksheet on page 51
- Participation in the discussion about heroes
- A reflective poem about a real-life hero

■ Extensions

- The students can write letters to their heroes, telling them how they have influenced their lives.
- Students can create awards, certificates, or medals for their heroes.

My Very Own Hero

My hero is with me always,
Running interference for the conflicts in my
    life.
My hero never lets me down,
Even during those moments when I don't
    return the favor.
Sometimes my hero watches me silently,
Allowing me to fall flat on my face.
There are times that I want to:
Cry,
Laugh,
Love,
Remember,
Sigh,
Lie,
Run away or repair old wrongs.
Those are the times when my hero speaks
    to me and helps me to decide the right
    thing to do.
My hero is a good friend.
My hero is my conscience.
My hero is ME, MYSELF, and I!

My Dad

My hero is my Dad.
He is the rock in my world
and the pillow of my sleep.
He is the Cadillac of my highway
    and the lighthouse of my travels.
My dad is the Superman of comic books
And the train engine that keeps me on the
    right track.
He is the bandage that mends all hurts
    and the computer disk of all I need to
    know.
My dad, my hero!

Dad

He is the one I admire most,
He never really boasts.
He taught me the way to live,
And helped me walk and talk.
Though he didn't do all the work,
He did a lot for me to admire him.
He is my Dad,
The one I admire, admire.
                    by Patrick Tucker

Grandma
Cool-headed, dependable,
Assisting, comforting, contributing,
Gladly giving her time,
Volunteer.

❖ *Hero*

Heroes of the Past

Write the names of heroes from the past. These people should have been recognized for various achievements and accomplishments.

1. _____
2. _____
3. _____
4. _____
5. _____
6. _____
7. _____
8. _____
9. _____

Present Day Heroes

Write the names of contemporary heroes. These should be selected based on your definition of a hero.

1. _____
2. _____
3. _____
4. _____
5. _____
6. _____
7. _____
8. _____
9. _____

Unsung Heroes

Write the names of your personal heroes – people who have never been recognized for their achievements but who serve as role models for you. You must personally know or have known them.

1. _____
2. _____
3. _____
4. _____
5. _____
6. _____
7. _____
8. _____
9. _____

Directions

✨ Choose one of your unsung heroes.

✨ Write a poem about this person.

✨ Use your poem to tell why this person is a hero to you.

✨ Your poem can be any length and any format, but you should use at least one poetic device.

First or Last Liners

Overview

The students will write poetry based on given first or last lines. The lines may be creative or taken from well-known poetry.

Objectives

- Students will select first and last lines for poems and write several possibilities the for story lines.
- Students will create poems based on the first and last lines.

Materials

- ✓ paper
- ✓ pens or pencils
- ✓ copies of pages 53 and 54

Procedure

There are several ways to use this lesson plan:

Option 1

This technique may be used to study well-known poetry. By using first and last lines as an introduction, each student will be forced to interpret or evaluate his or her thoughts about possible meanings of the poem without first reading the <u>entire</u> poem.

1. Give students the beginning or ending lines of a poem. Have them write several ideas for possible meanings of the poem. Once they have selected one of these, they should write a poem, somewhat in the same style of the author's first line shown to them.

   Note: No first and last lines from well-known published poetry are given in this lesson plan. You may select lines from poems found in textbooks or other resources for poetry.

2. Once students have completed writing their own poetry, they should read, study, and evaluate the original poems. Students can then compare their interpretations with the real meanings of the poems written by the actual famous authors.

Option 2

1. You may pre-select one line from the list on page 54. Students should then pre-write some possible story lines for their poems, select the one they like the most, and write their poems.

2. Since everyone is using the same first line, these should be read aloud to see how many unique possibilities were generated by the class.

Evaluation

- Exploration of different possibilities to find meaning for the first and last lines
- Poem that reflects a plausible meaning of the first or last lines

Extension

- Ask students to write a first line for a poem, then have them trade with other members of the class. Then they can write poetry based on someone else's first line.

A First Line Poem

It was a blissful day, a union of the sun and earth...
The blazing solar giant bathed her skin in golden tones
And burnished it copper,
With a hint of glorious bronze.
Her hair was spread on a pillow of sand,
The golden locks made brighter with the sun.
Massive sunglasses reflected white-capped waves
Making their way to shore,
And the warm sand made a delicious respite
For her windswept body.
A palm tree swayed gently in the breeze,
As if dancing to the sweet melodious sounds of the music
Playing from within a nearby restaurant.

A Last Line Poem

The day was lovely and the group stood calmly,
    Together.
One head bounced up and looked around,
    Nothing.
Another looked slowly around,
    Uneasily.
Several more began to shift their bodies,
    Nervously.
One small one crept closer to its mother,
    Clinging.
The sky turned dark and the sound of thunder was heard,
    Distantly.
When all of a sudden the leader belted out a warning...
    Moo-oo-ve!
And the herd of peaceful cows was suddenly electrified!

Use these phrases as a first line for a poem or as the last line of a poem.

- The raindrops fell, like granite tears…
- The situation deserves a much closer look…
- No doubt about it…
- The simple things in life are near at hand…
- Take time to fly…
- In the silvery light of a moonlit night…
- I am but one in this world…
- He was a warm and cuddly, soft and furry bandit…
- The moment stood breathtakingly still…
- There was an eternity of silence…
- A small life, yet a great endeavor…
- A witness to the great event, he (she) felt a moment of freedom …
- Crowds of city people paused as one to ponder…
- Bubbling over with enthusiasm for the day, I…
- I, like the mighty wind, am destined for…
- The herd of peaceful cows was suddenly electrified…
- Fear was thine enemy…
- The day was blissful, a union of the sun and earth…
- It was a whimsical song, its plaintive sound brought forth by a gentle breeze…
- He was a rock-solid man of the earth…
- A lovely child, a beautiful woman…
- A small body of warmth, sure to bring laughter…
- The jingling sounds from a distance…
- When one hath no other, what is one to do?…
- Advice to a child…
- A curious eagle flew closer to take a look…
- The perpetual motion of a young life…
- Such diversity it was - the handsome man (woman) and the ugly cockroach…
- The moment was sublime…
- A wrinkled old woman and a smooth-skinned young beauty…
- I am the future…
- Her (his) happiness knew no bounds…

Catch the Moment (a Sensory Poem)

Overview

The students write sensory poetry about an unplanned moment in time. The main purpose of this assignment is for the students to turn everyday, mundane activities into creative, descriptive poetry.

Objectives

- Students will participate in an activity that focuses on the use of sight, smell, and hearing.
- Students will list words encountered during the sensory activity.
- Students will write sensory poems based on the words from their lists.

Materials

- ✓ copies of page 56
- ✓ paper
- ✓ pens or pencils
- ✓ a quiet location without many distractions

Procedure

1. To successfully complete this activity, students will need a quiet place (not necessarily silent) where there are very few distractions. It is important to select a time of day when students least expect it to happen. Good times for this lesson would be a rainy day, a windy day, a thunderstorm, outside on cushions on a balmy spring day, an autumn day when leaves and pine cones are falling, or near the cafeteria during lunch time.

2. Instruct students to take out a sheet of paper and a pen or pencil. Ask them to put their heads down and close their eyes and listen and smell everything possible for a five-minute period of time.

3. At the end of the five minutes, ask students to write all of the things they smelled or heard when their eyes were closed. Then allow students another couple of minutes to write everything they see in the location.

By this time, all students should have a list of several words and/or phrases to be used in their poetry. Do not allow them to share their lists with one another because many of them will have experienced different sensory inputs.

4. Instruct students to write poems about their sensory experiences. These poems should be entitled "Catch the Moment" with the time of day and the weather as a subtitle.
Example:

Catch the Moment
Nine O'clock on a Rainy Friday Morning

The poetry should be written using similes and metaphors (example on page 56), and must contain at least two lines each about sight, smell, and hearing.

Evaluation

- Participate in a sensory listening and listing activity
- A poem that turns a mundane, everyday moment into a creative experience
- Use of sensory input in a poem
- Use of similes, metaphors, and personifications in a poem

Extensions

- Students can write a short story using the setting as described in their stories.
- Students can paint an abstract picture using colors that represent their sensory experiences.

Catch the Moment
On a Rainy Monday Morning in the School Cafeteria

The room is large, like a giant cavity,
Tables lined up like soldiers,
With the grand piano serving as officer in charge.
Quiet, with the occasional sound of voices,
And the rain gently drumming on the roof,
The cafeteria noises, trays banging,
People coughing in the distance,
Anxious for the week to end,
Bored with the same routine.
The smell of chalk dust and bubble gum,
A fruity smell — could it be raspberry?
The smell of a pencil eraser,
With just the faint aroma of coffee in the distance.

Catch the Moment
Sunset on a Summer Night

The birds sing their last songs,
Noisy frogs sit up and croon,
Chatty crickets join the chorus,
The sounds are staccato notes arranged
    at random.

The sky's a masterful painter,
Changing the rosy hues to blue,
It sprinkles stars on its canvas,
And carefully paints the moon.

The honeysuckle sheds its blanket,
A spray of sweet perfume,
Lilacs dip their heavy heads,
Like children ready to slumber.

A gentle breeze whisks by like a ghost
    in the night,
Kissing my cheek,
Hurrying on to other places.
I feel a storm approaching,
Slowly, silently,
Like a cat ready to attack.

Directions

✴ Spend five minutes paying close attention to everything around you, every noise, smell and sight.

✴ Take note of everything you see, smell and hear.

✴ Use these images to write a poem that lets the reader share your experience.

✴ Use similes and metaphors to enhance the images.

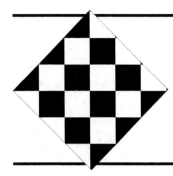

Chapter 4

Desserts

Poetry Ideas Topped With Art Activities

Do you find that you don't have time for teaching art? The perfect solution is to combine it with a writing experience. The lessons in this section let you incorporate a visual art experience in your language arts curriculum. With these innovative lessons art spurs poetic writing or is a vehicle for displaying or highlighting the poetry. Most of the poems may be written with any format, thus allowing the student more opportunities for creative interpretation. These mouth-watering poetry desserts are topped with art activities that will make those with a sweet tooth beg for more!

Wish You Were Here

◆ Overview

Students are to write a postcard-sized letter in a poetic format about a place that has made a great impression on them.

◆ Objectives

- Students will show creative use of similes or metaphors, color words, and vivid adjectives in their poems.
- Students will design pictures of the special places on one side of a large index card.

◆ Materials

- ✓ index cards
- ✓ pens and pencils
- ✓ watercolors, markers, colored pencils, or crayons
- ✓ paper for the rough draft
- ✓ a computer for word processing (optional)

◆ Procedure

1. Ask students to select a place that they find especially appealing and write a number of words or phrases that describe these special places.

2. Explain to students that they are to write a postcard poem about this favorite place that is at least four stanzas long. The poem should contain the following elements:
   - two or three similes or metaphors
   - vivid adjectives
   - two or three color words
   - some reference as to how this special place makes you feel emotionally

3. Students will then write a rhymed or non-rhymed poem that can fit on a postcard and be sent to a real or imaginary person. The poem will consist of several elements that vividly describe a place they have visited or they wish to see in the future. The format is as follows:
   - The first line will say "Dear_____," and the second line will say "Wish you were here!" These lines are separate from the poem itself.
   - The rest of the poem is loosely formatted but must include the elements listed above.

4. Students should then type or print neatly their poems on a small sheet of paper.

◆ Art Activity

1. The students will create a picture of their special places on the unlined side of a large index card. Each picture should show all of the colors and descriptions from the poems.

2. On the back, students are to separate the card with a vertical line drawn from top to bottom. One side should be wider, allowing for the typed poem. On the right hand side of the card, a real or fictional address should be written and a creative stamp placed in the upper corner.

◆ Evaluation

- Poem that includes metaphors, similes, colors, and vivid adjectives
- Appropriate accompanying artwork
- Use of descriptive words

◆ Extension

- Create stationery with designs from favorite places. Use stamps or watercolors to design them.

Dear Mary,

Wish you were here!

Pensacola. Where the brilliant golden-orange
    sun sends its warming rays
In all their glorious splendor
To bask on the crest of the beautiful,
    crystal clear ocean.

At the close of day
The sea is a dolphin,
Balancing the sun like a ball on its silvery nose,
Its waves like tentacles,
Reaching out to grasp its many colors
As the day slowly ends.

To:

Mary Jones
1314 Spring Circle
Chicago, IL 60502

Pensacola, a quiet place, beautiful and warm,
Bringing a sense of peace and happiness
To all those who visit!

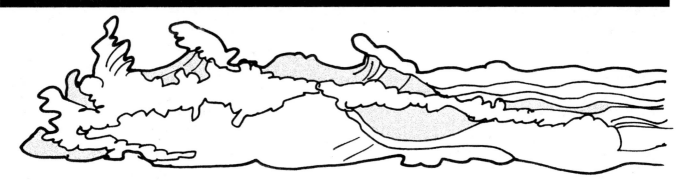

Directions

- ⊙ Choose a favorite place.
- ⊙ Write a poem to describe this place.
  The poem should be at least four stanzas long.
- ⊙ The poem should include:
  - · two to three similes or metaphors
  - · vivid adjectives
  - · two or three color words
  - · some reference as to how this place makes you feel

Sweety Gram

Overview

Students will create fun-to-eat poetry that is appropriate to give as an award or a gift to someone else. It is fun to make and delicious to receive because it consists of humorous verses and real-life candy and gum. This is a good activity to do after Halloween when students have an ample supply of candy.

Objectives

- Students will demonstrate the ability to write a rhyming poem about a specific person, incorporating different names of candy (to express physical and personality characteristics) into each verse of the poem.

- Students will design the Sweety-Gram poetry on a large sheet of tag board or poster board, using attractive lettering or computer graphics, and will tape the candy or candy bars in the appropriate places on the board.

Materials Needed

- ✓ paper
- ✓ poster board
- ✓ candy
- ✓ markers
- ✓ double-stick tape
- ✓ copies of page 61

Procedure

1. As a class, make a list of different kinds of candy and gum.

2. Once there is a long enough list, ask each student to write a poem to someone they know, incorporating names of candy in each of the verses. There should be a minimum of three verses and each verse should contain a rhyming scheme (AABB or ABAB).

3. Once students have completed the poems, they should write them on sheets of poster board, leaving spaces for the actual candies. Each student is to bring in his or her own candy to complete the poem, and should use double-sided tape to stick them in the proper places on the poster board.

Art Options

Option 1
Computer graphics or original artwork should be used on the poster to enhance the looks of the project.

Option 2
Another presentation option would be to put the poem in a booklet form. The booklet can be made by cutting poster board or tag board into letter size sheets and writing different verses on each page. The candy should be taped in place, and the entire booklet should be tied together with yarn or ribbon.

Note: You may prefer to use wrappers only for this option as actual candy is too bulky to incorporate into a book.

Evaluation

- A poem that relates a person's characteristics to various candies

- Use of rhyme

- Attractive presentation

Directions

Write a poem to a friend or family member using the names of candy, gum, or candy bars to describe his or her personal characteristics. The poem should have four stanzas and should rhyme. In your final presentation, put the candy (or wrappers) in place of the candy names.

To Lydia, my best friend:

You are such a "Sweetart"™
It can be said,
Even if at times
You're just an "Airhead"™.

You're a real "Laffy Taffy"™
And lots of fun,
A true "Jolly Rancher"™
If ever there was one.

Your hair is so blond,
It's "Alpine White"™,
Your thoughts are in the "Milky Way"™,
Far out of sight.

You're just a "Butterfingers"™
When you stumble and fall,
But you're a real "Almond Joy"™
For one and for all.

Have a deliciously happy birthday!

Photographic Essay

■ Overview

Students participate in a photo hunt on the school campus, looking for unusual pictures. Then they write poetic essays based on these pictures.

■ Objectives

- Students will demonstrate creative thinking through the selection of shots taken on the photo hunt.
- Students will demonstrate an ability to take quality photo shots based on a list of assignments.
- Students will write a poetic photo essay.

■ Materials

- ✓ paper
- ✓ pens or pencils
- ✓ cameras and film
- ✓ copies of pages 63 and 64
- ✓ a sketchbook, a notebook, or poster board

■ Procedure

1. This writing/photo assignment can be an activity unto itself or part of a larger photography unit. Regardless of the depth of the study, it is important to introduce students to several important facts about taking good pictures. Prior to taking pictures, cover the following points with students:

   - **Composition** is extremely important. Tell students to look through the viewfinder to locate their best shots. It narrows down their field of vision and helps them to focus on more unique and detailed pictures.

   - **Be still.** Once students have their shots in the viewfinders they should keep the camera very still, hold their breaths, and hold their elbows close to their bodies while the shot is being taken.

   - **Watch out for shadows**. When photographing people, look very closely at where shadows fall on the faces. Sometimes a person's face will be distorted or details will be lost if the shadows are too intense.

   - **Know your camera.** Whether a student is using a disposable camera or one that has very expensive lenses, he or she should become aware of the capabilities of that camera. For example, most disposable cameras will not take clear pictures if they are closer than 4 to 5 feet from the subject.

   - **Be Creative**. Take time to look for the unique or unusual shot. Taking a picture of a common object from an unusual perspective can be dramatic.

2. Make copies of the student reproducible page and distribute them to all students. Give students cameras and encourage students to look for subjects that happen naturally and do not appear contrived. Encourage students to take their time to get the unusual or creative shots. Note: The subject of the pictures should not be people unless otherwise stated.

3. Once the pictures are developed, each student should pick out five to six best photos and paste them in either a journal sketchbook or on a large sheet of poster board. These pictures should be arranged in such a way that they tell a story about the location (for example, the school). Once the pictures are secured, students are to write a few lines of poetry about each one of the photos, telling a story in poetry essay form. Students may choose to use <u>all</u> of their pictures to build their poetic essays.

■ Evaluation

- High quality, creative photographs
- Descriptions of photos expressed poetically
- Attractive, interesting photo essay

These poems were excerpted from a couple of different poetic essays

Title: **Our School**

 Photo 1 - a picture of the school garbage dump

Crumpled old and smelly,
Rank and old,
This trash container
Reeks of spoiled milk and mold.

Photo 2 - a puddle of water with the sun reflected on its surface

A lovely reflection,
The sun shown below.
Its glorious colors,
Showing a beautiful, golden glow.

Photo 3 - a picture of a tree

On the horizon
The tree stands tall.
A majestic giant
That towers over us all.

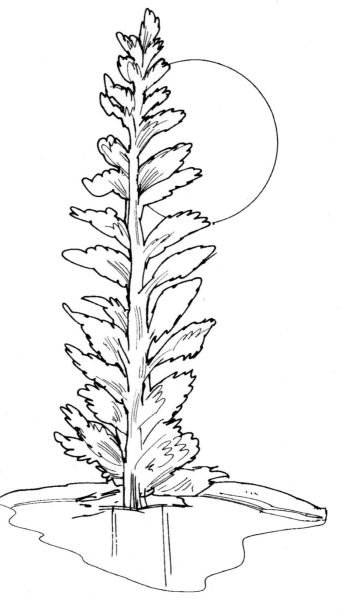

Photo 4 - a picture of the school building taken from the best possible vantage point

A large red brick structure
Sprawled out in the sun.
Oak Valley School
With its distant voices of learning and fun.

Photo 5 - a photo of a golf ball in the middle of the soccer field

Out on the soccer field
Nestled on a grassy mound,
A small Wilson golf ball
Just waits to be found.

Directions for Photos

Using the list below, find creative ways to photograph the school campus. Do not take any pictures of people unless the directions tell you to do so. Most of the pictures should be of accidental happenings and should not be purposely set up. Some of the pictures should show man-made objects in a creative way. Take the time to compose your photographs to take advantage of the best lighting and perspective.

Take pictures of the following:

- something that is ugly
- something that is beautiful
- something that is humorous in nature
- a creative shot of a tree
- the school building, shown from a unique perspective
- something in nature that is unusual for a school campus
- something manmade that is unusual for a school campus
- a scenic view of the campus without the school building
- something that represents peace and harmony
- a shot that includes one or two people
- a picture of "eyes"
- a dazzling smile

Directions for Poetry

✎ Choose several of your best photographs that can be combined to tell a story about the location or that develop a theme.

✎ Write a poem that has four lines describing each picture.

✎ Use descriptive language.

✎ Use either an ABCB and an ABAB rhyme pattern.

Dr. Seuss Junk Critter

◆ Overview

The students will design a critter from junk items and write poetry in the style of Dr. Seuss. This project may be developed independently or with a small group.

◆ Objectives

- Students will design and name creatures made of junk items.
- Students will read and study the writing style of Dr. Seuss.
- Students will develop poetry stories in the style of Dr. Seuss, using their junk critters as the subject of the poems.

◆ Materials

- ✓ paper
- ✓ pens and pencils
- ✓ hot glue gun, glue sticks, rubber cement or liquid glue (your choice)
- ✓ a variety of junk items
- ✓ copies of page 66

◆ Procedure

1. Give students access to junk items and ask them to design critters out of the materials provided. The critters should consist of a minimum of six different items and must include eyes, feet, and arms or wings. The critters must also have names and histories (see the student reproducible sheet). Give students 30 minutes to create their critters. Once the critters are constructed, students can name them.

2. Spend some time reading Dr. Seuss books, such as *The Cat in the Hat, Green Eggs and Ham,* or *Horton Hatches the Egg.* Most of the older students will enjoy going back to their childhoods to read some of their favorite Dr. Seuss books. As they read them, encourage everyone to pay careful attention to the rhythm and rhyming patterns used by Dr. Seuss. When they finish several of the stories, discuss the characteristics of Dr. Seuss's writings.

3. Have students write story poems about their critters in the style of Dr. Seuss's writing.

4. Once the critters and stories have been completed, have students present their projects to the other members of the class.

◆ Evaluation

- Creative, attractive critter
- Poem that tells a story and reflects the writing style of Dr. Seuss
- Entertaining presentation

◆ Extensions

- Students may opt to write their story poems in book form with colorful illustrations and creative covers.
- The critters can be made of clay and shown as a computer "claymation" presentation.
- Several students may join together and combine their individual critters into a collaborative story poem using all of the group's characters.

Candace

A little junk critter name Candace LaRue
Wore a cowboy boot and a beaten-up shoe.
Her body was made of an old spray bottle
And her arms and hair were stuck on with glue

Said Candace one day to her junkyard crew
"I'm tired of this old ugly shoe!
I want a boot to match the other,
A shiny one that looks like new."

Her friends all groaned and sighed a lot...
"Candace, can't you be happy with what you've got?"
"No!" yelled Candace, "It doesn't look right
An old shoe with a boot is a most ugly sight!"

The more she fussed, her frustration grew
And her friends were annoyed and said they were through.
One boy stopped and screamed to the crowd
"We'll never have peace
All because of that lousy shoe!"

Candace screamed real loud
And she pulled at her hair
"I want another boot!
It's just not fair!"

But that very same boy had more things to say
So everyone listened and let him have his way.
"Listen to me...I have a solution.
I have an answer...I have resolution.
Candace needs a boot or she'll drive us all crazy.
Let's all work together. Let's not be lazy.
If we put forth the effort and search very hard
We might find another boot in this old junkyard."

So they searched and they looked all over the place
And they found a matching boot in a near-by space.
"Oh my goodness," said Candace, "now I'll need a new suit!"
The whole group sighed and they gave her the boot!

Making Your Critter

Design a junk critter using at least six of the materials given to you by your teacher. Include the following:

◎ eyes
◎ arms or wings
◎ feet (legs are optional, but your critter must be able to freely stand)
◎ a name for the critter
◎ a written history - include its origin, language, customs, or favorite sayings
◎ something that adds color

Writing Your Poem

✎ Take all of the information that you have invented about your creature and write a creative, funny poem that uses the writing style of Dr. Seuss.

✎ The poem should be in story form and should have a definite rhyme and rhythm.

✎ Plan a way to display your poem with your critter.

Sun Scene

Overview

After reading Ray Bradbury's short story, *All Summer in a Day*, the students will discuss the story in depth and talk about a time when the sun/sunrise/sunset was important to them.

Objectives

- Students will read *All Summer in a Day*, by Ray Bradbury and participate in a class discussion about the story.
- Students will write poems that reflect their experiences in the sun.
- Students will create three-dimensional sun/sunset/sunrise scenes and write their poems on the scenes.

Materials

✓ copies of *All Summer in a Day* by Ray Bradbury
✓ paper
✓ pens and pencils
✓ construction paper, cardboard
✓ glue, hot glue
✓ glitter and unusual papers

Story Synopsis

In the story, *All Summer in a Day*, a young girl has moved to the planet Venus where it rains all of the time and the sun only comes out once every seven years. Margot remembers the sun from having lived on Earth. The other children in her class do not believe the things that she remembers about the sun, and they constantly make fun of her. On the day the sun is to come out Margot is busy describing the sun and comparing it to things like a penny. The other children become very annoyed with her all-knowing ways, and they lock her in a closet right before the sun comes out. They play and enjoy the full glory of the sun. It only lasts an hour, and the rain starts to fall once again. When they all run inside the building, they suddenly remember that Margot had been locked in the closet.

Procedure

1. Read the story *All Summer in a Day*. When the students have finished reading the story, allow no discussion until each person has written down at least three questions about the story. Encourage students to ask open-ended questions, questions that could not be truly answered unless they were asked of the author himself.

2. Group the students in a circle. Instruct them to direct all questions to one another instead of the teacher. You can ask the first question, and the group will follow by asking and responding to each others' questions.

3. After the discussion of the story, have the students make lists of their own special moments in the sun. After narrowing down the individual lists, each should select his or her favorite, most vivid memory and write a descriptive paragraph about it. After completing these paragraphs, students are to extract ideas that they can put into a poem. There is no specific format for this poetry assignment, but the lines of the poem should be more descriptive and rhythmic than sentences students used to write the paragraphs.

4. Finally, students will design a three-dimensional shadow box or relief picture that illustrates the poetry. They should use a variety of colors and materials in the three-dimensional project.

5. They should then write the lines of their poems on the three-dimensional projects.

Evaluation

- A creative, descriptive poem.
- A three-dimensional project that uses a variety of materials.

The Sunset

The evening sun bathes the valley
    in brilliant rays,
And the glorious yellows, oranges, pinks and reds,
Slowly fade to a watercolor rainbow.
The majestic mountains darken to a purplish hue,
A whimsical waterfall rushes quickly to the
    shimmering river below.
Suddenly, the lingering light fades like a pair of
    stonewashed jeans,
And darkness reigns.

Sun

The lovely lady sun
Had on a liquid dress
Shrouded over in purple chiffon -
The early morning mist.

Her bonnet of red passion
Resting upon her bronze-tinted hair
Was tied loosely in the latest fashion
So her locks cascaded everywhere.

With lips of delicate scarlet
She kissed the lavender sky
Spreading soft light in a fragile net
And letting gentle warmth fly.
by Hannah Huff

Too Hot!

Morn is born,
Warm, balmy,
It beckons us to play.
    Dancing,
    Prancing,
    Racing,
Under the sun.

Noon, too soon,
Blazing, fiery,
It showers its peppery spray,
    Scorching,
    Torching
    Searing,
Under the sun.

Seeking shade,
Cool, refreshing,
It shields with a comforting canopy.
    Soothing,
    Moderating,
    Softening,
The heat of the sun.

Abstract Concepts

■ Overview

Students create poetry that symbolizes one of several abstract concepts and create three-dimensional sculptures that represent the concepts presented in their poems.

■ Objectives

- Students will brainstorm words or phrases that represent a selected topic.
- Students will write poems that elaborate on the meaning of the selected topics.
- Students will make sculptures out of junk that depict their selected theme.

■ Materials

✓ pens or pencils
✓ paper
✓ various junk items, including scraps of wood and nature materials like stones, nuts, and leaves
✓ hot glue and glue gun
✓ scissors, rulers

■ Procedure

1. Begin by discussing the difference between abstract and concrete. An abstract concept is an expression of a characteristic but is not connected to any specific, real object or action. Concrete, on the other hand, means an actual thing; something that is real or dealing with reality. Love is an abstract idea, but a kiss is a concrete thing.

2. Give students a choice of the following topics or add topics of your choosing:

· power	· love
· courage	· happiness
· beauty	· power
· violence	· communication
· cooperation	· truth
· wisdom	· progress
· justice	· change
· emotion	· liberty
· goodness	· honor

3. Then give students time to write words, phrases, or sentences pertaining to the abstract topic they have selected. In addition to listing synonyms and descriptive phrases, they will need to provide concrete examples of their abstract themes.

4. Ask students to combine the words and phases into poems. The poems can be any length and any format. You may want to let them put their poems aside while they work on the art portion of this lesson and come back to poems after they have dealt with the topic in a different format. At this point, they may wish to revise their poems.

■ Art Project

5. Have students design three-dimensional sculptures to depict their chosen themes. The sculptures should have several symbols that are associated with the selected topics. First have them design the sculptures on paper. The designs should include the following:
   - There should be 8 to 10 words, phrases, pictures or symbols that are related to the selected topics.
   - The sculptures should have a base.
   - The words or symbols should be on all sides of the sculptures.

6. Have students make the sculptures out of junk materials.

7. The poems should be displayed with the sculptures.

Alternative Project

Instead of three-dimensional sculptures students can make posters by cutting out and mounting pictures and words that represent the topic of their poems. The poems can be incorporated into the posters.

■ Evaluation

- A poem that gives meaning to the abstract topic selected
- A three-dimensional sculpture that depicts the chosen topic

War

Looming clouds of darkness,
And anxious beating hearts,
Thundering in the background.
From a great distance, many watchful eyes
See many things.
The cost is dear –
Bloodshed,
Sadness,
Victors, losers,
The many victims.
The sun breaking forth at the end of day,
And peace reigns slowly across the span of time.

Beauty

If beauty were a tree,
She would be a pine,
Feather-like branches
Strong, sturdy spine.

If beauty were a flower,
She would be a rose,
Perfectly shaped,
Pleasing to the nose.

If beauty were a landscape,
She would be the ocean,
Silvery, shifting sands,
Waves, tossed and spun.

If beauty were an animal,
She would be a deer,
Gentle, silent creature,
Free roaming the frontier.

If beauty were a vehicle,
She would be a Jaguar,
Sleek, shiny, swift,
The perfect sports car.
　　　　　by Jaimee Frankian

Directions

❊ Select an abstract concept.

❊ Write words and phrases that are related to this topic or that are concrete depictions of this idea.

❊ Combine these ideas into a poem. Your poem can be any length and any format but it should include several thoughts that demonstrate this abstract idea.

❊ Make a three-dimensional sculpture that also depicts this topic.

❊ Display your art project and poem together.

Poetry Wall

◆ Overview

The students will write short meaningful poems that will be displayed on a wall in the classroom. This is a project that can extend over a long period of time.

◆ Objectives

- Students will write short verses about meaningful topics.
- Students will display the poetry on a wall in the classroom.
- Students will design illustrations to accompany the poetry.

◆ Materials

✓ a bulletin board or a long sheet of bulletin board paper hung on the wall.
✓ black markers
✓ crayons, oil pastels, colored markers or watercolor paint
✓ copies of page 72

◆ Procedure

1. Designate a bulletin board or wall in your classroom for displaying students' poetry. If you wish, you can use a large piece of paper that you have colored to look like bricks. This bulletin board should remain up for a long period of time and should be added to consistently.

2. Collect samples of students' poems from various poetry assignments. These assignments should be done over a period of time. You should assign at least one or more poems each week that are written on paper or in student journals. After the poems have been evaluated for quality and appropriateness they may be placed on the poetry wall.

3. When students have been approved to write their poems on the wall, they may write them using whatever materials are available, and they should draw or paint pictures or symbols to accompany each poem. They must sign their names to the poems.

◆ Evaluation

- Short, meaningful poem that contains a good rhyming scheme.
- Art or symbols that enhance or emphasize the poem

Friendships are special,
Friendships are great,
Friendships are something
To appreciate.

What shall I be
What will the future hold
Will I be rich
Before I am old?

Shall I seek my fortune
Travel over this earth
And be an adventurer
To find my true worth?

It's fun to be popular
But it can hurt, too
Because nothing's a secret
When someone talks about you!

Grades are a problem
Almost every day
They get you grounded
With no time to play

If you work very hard
And you manage a "C"
Your mom is still angry
'Cause she wanted a "B."

You try to explain
That you don't understand "math"
But she said you didn't try
And you still feel her wrath.

Directions

Choose one of the topics listed to the right. Write a short poem about the topic. Your poem should rhyme, but you can use any format. When you are finished, design art that will enhance your poem and have your teacher post the poem and artwork on the poetry board.

Topics
✓ school
✓ friendships
✓ parties
✓ grades
✓ popularity
✓ parents
✓ hobbies
✓ sports
✓ the future

Artful Poetry

Overview

Students will respond to a famous painting by writing poetry that reflects the perspective of the artist and one of the subjects in the paintings, and they will paint or draw a picture in the artist's style.

Objectives

- Students choose their favorite paintings and collect information about the artist.
- Students will write poems about their favorite paintings.
- Students will create a picture in the same style as the one they chose to write about in their poems.

Materials

- ✓ pens or pencils
- ✓ writing paper, drawing paper
- ✓ charcoal pencils, watercolors, or crayons
- ✓ available art reference materials
- ✓ copies of page 74

Procedures

1. Have available or instruct students to look up pictures of these ten paintings.
   - *Mona Lisa* by Leonardo da Vinci
   - *American Gothic* by Grant Wood
   - *Lyric (Man on a Horse)* by Wassily Kandinsky
   - *Breezing Up* by Winslow Homer
   - *Three Musicians* by Pablo Picasso
   - *Self-Portrait* by Vincent Van Gogh
   - *Sunday Afternoon on the Island of Grand Jatte* by Georges Seurat
   - Norman Rockwell paintings

2. After the students have located all of the pictures, they should study them carefully and select one that appeals to them. Play soothing classical music while students write thoughts and short descriptions that represent their reactions to the paintings.

3. After about ten minutes, allow them to discuss and evaluate the paintings. During this discussion ask some of the following questions:
   - Why do you think the artist painted this picture?
   - What do you think the picture represents? Is there some symbolism or message that is conveyed?
   - Who are the people in the painting? Why were these people selected as the subjects of the painting?
   - What is the subject in the painting thinking at the time the picture was painted?

4. At the conclusion of the discussion, have each student conduct research about his or her selected artist and painting. Notes should be taken, but no formal paper will be written.

5. Then have students take all the factual information, combine it with their impressions, and write poems. The poems should be written in two parts.
   - One section will consist of the thoughts of the artist who painted the picture.
   - The other verse of the poem will reflect the thoughts and feelings of someone or something in the painting itself.

6. Once the poems have been written, each student is to draw or paint a picture in the same style as the artist. Both the poem and the artwork should be displayed together.

Evaluation

- Ability to research
- Poem that presents two different viewpoints – the artist and one of the subjects in the painting
- A picture in the same style as the artist studied

73

Leonardo da Vinci (speaking)

Mona Lisa, Mona Lisa
Men have named you
But that should not be true
If only they really knew…
The world pays homage to your beauty,
What a laugh we would all enjoy
If they realized that Mona Lisa was a boy!
A mystery surrounds you all the while
You, with those roving eyes and secret smile
I just can't risk my reputation
By confessing that I painted myself
　from a reflection
Oh Mona, Mona, should I confess
That you are me?
Oh what a mess!

Mona Lisa (speaking)

Oh Leonardo, you silly oaf,
Why do you worry me with your woes?
Why did you allow yourself to pose,
And why did you paint me with such an ugly nose?
Why couldn't you have been patient
And found a model to sit?
Or were you afraid that she might quit?
Instead, you decided to paint your own face,
And now you have to contend with questions
　from the human race.
Oh Leonardo, Leonardo, why do you care?
Someday this picture will be valuable,
A painting so rare.

Directions

Carefully study a painting by a famous artist. Also find as much information about this artist as you can. Then combine your observations and the factual information into a poem. The poem will have two parts. One part will reflect on the possible thoughts of the artist. The other part will present the thoughts of someone or something in the painting. Your poem may be in any format.

Put It to Music

Overview

Students write about a variety of topics in the form of songs and present them as CDs, cassette tapes or records.

Objectives

- Students will write facts about a selected topic or about a unit that has been studied.
- Students will write poems that incorporates their knowledge of the subject.
- Students will write poems in the form of songs (any style).
- Students will create an attractive graphic design for an album cover, a CD case or a cassette tape case.

Materials

✓ paper
✓ pens and pencils
✓ cardboard or tagboard
✓ blank cassette tapes in their plastic boxes and blank CDs and empty CD cases
✓ markers, paint, colored chalk, construction paper, and glitter
✓ optional: old record album covers and records

Procedure

1. Assign a subject for the writing assignment or let students choose a topic. As a group have students create a thought web of words or phrases associated with the topic. Some possible themes are:

- love
- school
- friends
- nature
- family
- money
- war
- a literary character
- something you have recently studied
- time
- change
- sports
- knowledge
- transportation
- entertainment
- a country

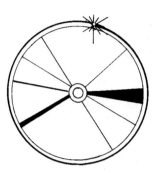

2. Then have students take the ideas from the group session and write songs on this theme. They should have at least three verses in their songs, and the lyrics should provide information about the subject. The poems/songs do not have to rhyme, but they should have a regular rhythm that could be set to music.

Art Project

3. Students should then select a format for presenting their songs. They can choose a CD, a record or a cassette tape.

   The records and CDs can be made the exact size as a large record or regular CD by tracing them on cardboard or tag board. The cassette lyrics should also be written on a piece of paper that is folded and inserted into the cassette case. Students may record their songs if they wish.

4. Finally, instruct students to design visually-appealing album, CD, or cassette covers. They can write their names as song producers somewhere on the cover design.

Evaluation

- The poem/song gives important information about the assigned subject
- Poem uses appropriate rhyme and rhythm
- Cover is visually pleasing

Illinois

Illinois,
The land of Lincoln,
A northern mid-western state.
Illinois,
Home of Chicago,
Where tall buildings abound.
Illinois,
Fields of juicy sweet corn,
And miles of farm lands.
Illinois,
Located at the top of Lake Michigan,
Neighbor of Iowa and Indiana.
Illinois,
A beautiful state,
With its historical capital, Springfield.

The County Fair

We went to the county fair,
Not knowing what would be there.
We gawked in surprise,
We examined the size,
Of the twelve-pound prize-winning hare.
Oh the county fair, the county fair,
Everything's there at the county fair.

We went to the county fair,
With plenty of money to spare,
We rode all the cool rides,
Ate until we were cross-eyed.
And quit when our wallets were bare.
Oh the county fair, the county fair,
Everything's there at the county fair.

We went to the county fair,
Hoping to see something rare,
A horse that could croon,
A man playing a spoon,
A sheep that could walk up a stair.
Oh the county fair, the county fair,
Everything's there at the county fair.
　　　by Ben Lower

Directions

- Choose a topic of interest. Collect information about this topic.
- Use your information to write a poem that could be set to music. The poem can be any format. It does not have to rhyme, but it should use rhythm or repetition.
- One format you could use is:
  ✓ line 1 - one word that is the topic of the poem
  ✓ line 2 and 3 - information about the topic
  ✓ line 4 - repeat the topic word
  Repeat this pattern.
- When you have finished, write your poem on a piece of cardboard that looks like a record, CD or cassette tape.
- Then create an attractive CD cover, album cover, or cassette cover to go with your poem.

Different Perspectives

◆ Overview

In this lesson, students are asked to write poetry that reflects childhood memories and shows two points of view.

◆ Objectives

- Students will free-write informal memory stories about incidents from their lives.
- Students will write the same stories from the viewpoint of another person or thing.
- Students will develop poems taken from the free-writing exercise.

◆ Materials

✓ pencils and pens
✓ writing paper
✓ drawing paper
✓ colored pens, crayons, or paints

◆ Procedure

1. Ask students to relax, put their heads down, and close their eyes as you read the story on page 78 about an early morning experience.

    Note: You may, if you prefer, use one of your own life's stories for an example.

2. Conduct a class discussion in which students talk about the different emotions and feelings portrayed by the author of the story. Ask students to name other people, living things, or inanimate objects found in the story that might also be considered one of the main characters. As there are no other people mentioned, it is an obvious choice for students to name the doe as one of the major characters in the story. Some children may come up with more creative choices such as the baby fawn, a bird in a tree, some other forest animal, a stone or a dead branch stepped on by the deer.

3. Ask students to remember an incident or moment when they experienced something that was profoundly moving to them. Tell them to write about the incident from two perspectives, one from their own point of view and the other from the eyes of another character in the story. The story should be loosely constructed; just a pre-writing tool, not a formal draft.

4. Once the stories have been completed, write them in poetic form. The first part of the poem should be from the perspective of the student and the second part from another character's viewpoint. The poem should be shorter and use more vivid, succinct language than the prose version of the story.

◆ Art Project

5. Once the poems have been completed, have students fold a large piece of drawing paper in half. On one half of the paper they should draw a picture of their memories of the incident. On the other half they will draw a picture of the second person's viewpoint.

    Alternative Project

    The drawings can depict a window with two panes, one showing the student's perspective and one showing the other person's (thing's) perspective. Mount these pictures with a final copy of the poem.

◆ Evaluation

- Descriptive stories and poems presenting two perspectives of an experience
- Participation in group discussions
- Drawings that represent the two perspectives

◆ Extensions

- Students can design dioramas in which they show a scene about which they have written.

A Memory Story

I awakened in the early morning darkness of my parents' cabin. I could see the gradually graying of the sky in the east; unable to return to sleep, I grabbed a novel and made my way to the recliner in the living room. Curling up with a woolen afghan, I contemplated the wall of silence surrounding me, a silence that was broken only by the ticking of a clock. Heavy-lidded and at peace with the day, I found that I had no desire to read. Closing my eyes momentarily, I became suddenly aware of a difference in the quality of light. The graying sky was making way for the pale blue and gold of a brilliance that was yet to come. I rose from the chair, went to the window, and stood in silent awe as a beautiful doe and two baby fawns, their reflections mirrored in the serene waters of the lake, frolicked unafraid on the lawn below. The sentinel doe, suddenly stopped and listened to the wind. Her nose twitched. She heard some unspoken warning, and she darted suddenly into the woods, her two fawns leaping right behind her, white tails erect.

Early Morning Poem

I awakened in the early morning darkness of the cabin
To a gradually graying sky in the east
And a thick wall of silence,
Broken only by the ticking of a clock.
I stood in silent awe as a beautiful doe and her two fawns
Frolicked unafraid on the lawn below,
Their reflections mirrored in the serene waters of the lake.
Suddenly the sentinel doe, ever watchful and on guard, stopped…
And conveying some secret signal,
She bounded suddenly into the woods,
Her two offspring leaping right behind her, white tails erect.

I nickered softly to my babies,
Commanding them to follow my lead
Onto a sloping, grassy hill
Where I watched them play and dance
By the shores of the beautiful lake.
We were joyful together and unafraid.
When suddenly, I had an uneasy feeling
That all was not well.
I felt the hair on my back rise,
And I sensed something in the air!
There was danger lurking nearby
And someone was watching us in our play.
I became frightened when I noticed the wooden dwelling high on the hill.
And signaling to my babies,
We ran quickly into the safety of the forest.

Amusement Park Ride

◆ Overview

In this project students will write a form of concrete poetry. In concrete poems, the words are written to reflect the subject of the poem. In this lesson, students will write poems in the shape of a fair, carnival, or amusement park ride.

◆ Objectives

- Students will write poems based on an amusement park ride.
- Students will create pictures of the ride and will write the words of the poems in the shape of the rides.
- Students will use descriptive language within the poems.

◆ Materials

✓ paper
✓ pens or pencils
✓ watercolor paints, colored pencils, or crayons
✓ black marking pens

◆ Procedure

Students in my home town enjoy the state fair every fall, and there is always a great deal of classroom discussion about it. This topic of conversation is unavoidable, so I created this assignment about the rides at the fair. It works well for amusement park rides, different attractions at Disney World, and small carnival rides. Students love this activity. The appeal of fair ride presented as concrete poetry allows them to relive the whole fair experience.

1. Review concrete poetry. See description and examples on page 113.

2. Ask each student to select a favorite ride and list several words or phrases that best describe the feelings, the movement, the special effects, and the sounds associated with it.

3. Have students write a poem that communicates the sensations one would experience in being on this ride.

4. Students should then draw a picture of the ride that fills up the entire page. They should include all of the surrounding sights in the pictures. After the drawing is complete, each student is to figure out how to write the poem, following the lines of the ride. Then they are to write the words with a black permanent marker on the picture.

◆ Evaluation

- Ability to write concrete poetry
- A pleasing, colorful picture of an amusement park ride
- Use of descriptive vocabulary in the poem

◆ Extensions

- Students may wish to record their poems on tapes, using onomatopoeia (words that sound like the sounds they name) at every opportunity.

- Concrete poetry may be used for many different events or activities across the curriculum. For example, a study of the early settlement of America might produce concrete poetry in the shape of the Mayflower. In geometry class, concrete poetry could be used to explain different shapes, and in science class concrete poetry could be used to describe an atom or the solar system.

The Batman

The Batman:
Exhilarating, frightening, looping.
It speeds along the track,
Through twists and bends,
Fast, scary, thrilling,
I hope this ride never ends.
The Batman

The Carousel

Ponies plopped on a disk like lollipops,
    Around and around it goes.
Dipping low then charging to the tiptop,
    Around and around it goes.
Colors swirl without order or stratus,
    Around and around it goes.
The calliope blares its gleeful chorus.
    Around and around it goes.
Chargers, prancers, stallions and mares,
    Around and around it goes.
Bear their riders with glee and fanfare,
    Around once more and then it slows.
        by Justin Wood

Directions

☺ Choose a favorite amusement park ride.

☺ Write a poem about this ride. Your poem can be any length. Use words and phrases that are descriptive and relate to the movements of the ride.

☺ Make a picture of the ride and write your poem on the picture so it follows the contours of the drawing.

Puzzling Poems

◆ Overview

Students write poetry on jigsaw pieces, cut the pieces apart, and display them.

◆ Objectives

- Students will write poems about puzzling things.
- Students will uniquely decorate jigsaw pieces.
- Students will consider solutions to questions concerning puzzling situations, things that fit together and/or how to fit in.

◆ Materials

✓ paper
✓ pencils and pens
✓ mat board, foam board, posterboard or cardboard
✓ paint, glitter, discontinued wallpaper books, sequins, jewels, beads, glitter glue and fabric
✓ scissors or box-cutters

◆ Procedure

1. Brainstorm each of the following topics:
   - Things that are puzzling in our lives
   - Things that we don't yet know
   - Things that fit together
   - Ways to fit in at school

   Allow at least a minute or two for brainstorming each of the categories. Once students have individually listed several answers, they are to write them on the board or a giant sheet of paper.

2. Then have students select one of the listed items and write a poem using it as the subject.

3. Give students a piece of stiff white paper and instruct them to divide the paper into five sections that link together like puzzle pieces. Each piece should be about the same size. After editing their poems, the poems should be written or typed on the individual puzzle pieces.

4. Students should then decorate each of the five puzzle pieces. Each piece can be colored separately, glittered, glued, sequined, etc. Let the creativity flow! Be careful not to cover any of the writing.

5. Select one of the following two options for displaying the jigsaw puzzle poem:
   - Glue the entire puzzle on a piece of cardboard, mat board, posterboard or foam board and cut the pieces apart. Place them in a small cardboard box, labeled with the name of the student and the topic of the poem on the box lid.
   - Cut out the puzzle pieces and glue them to an attractive hard-surfaced background such as mat board. They should be mounted in such a way that the poem is readable.

◆ Evaluation

- A poem about a subject related to the theme of puzzles
- An attractive puzzle
- Participation in the brainstorming process and class discussion

◆ Extensions

- Students may write "puzzle metaphors" about their lives.
- Students may write their poems on smaller puzzle pieces, using many pieces, and writing only one or two words at a time.

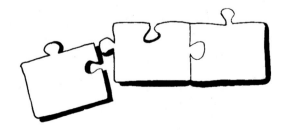

Puzzling Moments
Things that we don't yet know

Will the future bring me riches, money and gold?
Will I die very young or live to be old?
Will there be a cure for colds and the flu?
Will AIDS still exist or will there be something new?
Will my descendants colonize the Planet of Mars?
Will we travel in space to Milky Way stars?
Will oil wells run dry and cause us to falter?
Will Donald Trump make one more trip to the altar?
Will a woman be president of the U.S. of A.?
Or will students be learning a whole new way?
All of these things cause me to think and to ponder
And to worry about what will happen out yonder.
When will we know or have answers read?
One day soon, (hopefully) it will all be said.

People Puzzles

I always have to wonder,
I'm always asking why,
Some people give 100 percent,
And some people don't even try.
Some people are as nice as can be,
Some people are just plain mean,
Some people like to keep things loose,
Some people prefer routine.
Some people are so friendly,
They stop to ask how you feel,
Some people keep to themselves,
Their feelings they seldom reveal.
Some people are so quiet,
You rarely hear them talk,
Some people are the noisy sort,
They prattle, chatter and squawk.
People are a puzzle,
We're different as can be,
But without these distinctions,
There would be no variety.

Directions

✨ Write a poem about things you think are puzzling or about things that we don't know yet.

✨ On a piece of poster board draw a puzzle that has five pieces.

✨ Decorate each of the puzzle pieces.

✨ Write your poem on the puzzle pieces. Give it a title.

✨ Either cut the pieces apart and mount them on another piece of cardboard or put them in a box so others can put your puzzle poem together. Whichever way you decide to display your puzzle pieces, it should be easy for people to put them together and read your poem.

First Aid Poems

Overview

The students will write poetry about their positive traits and abilities to heal and help others. They will design large bandages and write this poetry on them.

Objectives

- Students will compile a list of their personality traits, talents and other abilities.
- Students will write poems about how they can be a comfort to others.
- Students will design a bandage or medicine container to showcase the poetry.

Materials

✓ paper
✓ pens or pencils
✓ copies of page 84
✓ computer (for typing the poetry)
✓ markers, paints

Procedure

1. Students will begin by listing their positive personality traits and abilities on a sheet of paper. Encourage them to list ways they are humorous and ways they help others.

2. Then have students use their lists to fill out the reproducible worksheet on page 84. This will be the framework for their poems. Students should think of all the ways they can heal or cure wounds; that is, ways they offer support and solace to others. They may interpret each of the categories as they wish and should feel free to add other important facts.

3. After analyzing the ways that they can be an aid to other people, they should structure their thoughts into a poem. The poems may take any format but should reflect their abilities to care and to make other people feel good.

4. Once the poems have been written, each student is to create a giant bandage or medicine bottle. On the bandage or bottle should be the brand name, a copy of the poem, the name of the student, and an attractive logo or design.

Evaluation

- A poem that reflects personal qualities and abilities to help others
- Self-knowledge
- Poem attractively displayed

Extensions

- Students may design boxes or packaging for their bandage poems.

Sample Poem

I am good for what ails you.
I can cure loneliness and sadness through...
   common sense,
   a caring attitude,
   and a finely-tuned sense of humor.
You would laugh at me
If you could have seen me...
   Dancing,
   Joke-telling,
   Falling on my face.
Use me to heal your wounds,
With a phone call or a visit.
Use me until you're happy again.
   Get well soon!

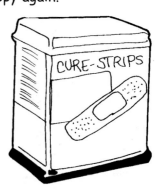

Let Me Help You Recuperate

How do you show other people you care? How do you make other people feel better? By answering these questions and completing these sentences, you will have the basics for a poem that tells how you help friends who are sick or feeling sad.

1. Start with a line like, **"I am good for what ails you."**

2. **I can cure** _____

   and _____
   (examples: sadness, loneliness, a bad mood, or a cold)

3. **With or by...**
   List three talents or three special things you can do.

   _____

   _____

   _____

4. **You would have laughed if you could have seen me.**
   Name three things that you have done or do regularly
   that are humorous and would make other people laugh.

   _____

   _____

   _____

5. **Give directions** for using your first aid.

   How often? _____

   Any precautions? _____

   Any extra advice? _____

6. **Finish the poem with a message** to the reader like "get well," "cheer up," or "smile."

7. After you have completed your poem, make a big bandage or medicine bottle and write your poem on it.

The Colors of My World

Overview

Students write poems that compare the colors of the earth to moments, occasions, or people in their lives.

Objectives

- Students will compare experiences in their lives to colors.
- Students use these comparisons to write poems.
- Students will design pages filled with the colors in their poems and then write the poetry with black marker over the graphic design.

Materials

✓ pencils or pens
✓ paper
✓ colored pencils, oil pastels, watercolor paints, crayons, markers, or torn construction paper pieces
  If students decide to use crayons or mosaic designs, the poem will have to be displayed to the side of the design.
✓ black marker
✓ heavy white drawing paper

Procedure

1. As a class, discuss the colors that are most commonly found in nature and list these on the board. Discuss how colors can affect our feelings or emotions and talk about the colors in nature and how they make us feel.

2. Ask students to list five of their favorite earth colors and write at least four or five experiences from their own lives that are related to those colors.

   To better guide them through this process, ask the following questions: "What are the reds in your life? the greens? the blues?

3. Students can then incorporate all of their color comparisons into color poems using any format they wish.

Art Project

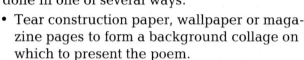

4. The art activity for this lesson is to create a visual palette or background of color to enhance the poetry. This may be done in one of several ways.

- Tear construction paper, wallpaper or magazine pages to form a background collage on which to present the poem.
- Paint or use oil pastels to create a background of all the colors in the poem. The design may be abstract or a realistic picture.
- Create mandalas (designs in circles) that incorporate all of the colors in the poem.
- Write the poem on part of the paper and add the design above, below or to the side of the design.

Evaluation

- A thoughtful, descriptive poem
- An attractive visual representation of colors in the poem
- Participation in class discussions

Extensions

- Students may write in a more specific way about life and nature. Instead of the assignment as described above, have them write about the colors of the ocean, the west, summer, evening, the zoo, their families, or love.

The Colors of My World

The colors of my world are:
Red, like the roses on the coffee table,
Red, like my sister's face when she is mad,
Red, like my brother's face after baseball practice,
Red, like the love I express on Valentine's Day.

Blue, like the crystal clear sky on a summer's day,
Blue, like my father's gentle eyes,
Blue, like a sparkling mountain lake,
Blue, like my favorite childhood toy.

Green, like freshly mowed grass after a gentle rain,
Green, like our Christmas tree lit up with white lights,
Green, like the garter snake that got into our kitchen,
Green, like my mother's emerald bracelet.

My Colors

Orange
Vibrant leaves in October,
Flames leaping from the fire,
Our lovable, hug-able cat,
Energizing, exciting,
An agitated color.

Green
The first trace of spring,
Fresh mown grass,
Soft molded hills,
Refreshing, restoring,
A tranquil color.

Yellow
Bright daffodils greeting the day,
Melt-in-your-mouth lemon pie,
Our sunlit kitchen,
Cheering, domineering,
A jubilant color.

Directions

🍁 Choose your favorite earth colors.

🍁 Make a list of experiences or feelings that are related to these colors.

🍁 Incorporate your best ideas into a poem about the colors of your world.

🍁 Your poem may be any format.

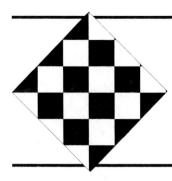

Chapter 5

Special Seasonings

Poetry for All the Seasons of the Year

Do you want a language lesson that is specifically for a holiday or special time of the year? This section provides ideas for poetry to highlight all the seasons of the year. Use these ideas throughout the year and you're guaranteed to add something extra to students' poetry writing skills. This section includes poems for the following themes or special days:

- Halloween
- Winter holidays
- Spring
- Patriotism
- Thanksgiving Day
- The past year
- Mother's Day
- Summer

Halloween

Overview

Students will select story elements and combine them to write scary Halloween poetry.

Objectives

- Students will write lines and dialogue based on pre-selected characters and a story starter given by the teacher.
- Students will create scary rhyming poems about Halloween.

Materials

✓ paper
✓ pens and pencils

Procedure

1. Read a scary poem like Edgar Allan Poe's *The Raven*. Discuss the poem. Tell students that they will be writing scary poetry. Each student will select from the following characters for his or her Halloween poem.

   - an animal
   - two people - a man and a woman, two best friends, a child and his or her grandmother or grandfather, or a child and one of his or her parents
   - an imaginary character – a ghost, a mummy, a vampire, or a witch
   - a setting - the woods at night, a deserted house, an empty beach, or an empty school

2. Once students have selected their cast of characters and a setting, they are to think of several different story lines for a story poem that connects all of these elements together. They can then select the best idea and write the poems.

Evaluation

- Selection of a cast of characters and a setting
- Development of a viable story line for the poem
- A poem that tells a Halloween story and incorporates rhyme

Extensions

- Students may write their stories in a short story format.
- Students may want to write poems about monsters. They should include at least three colors, the size of their monsters, and a description of its body and facial features.

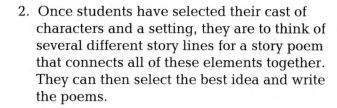

One Night at the School

Two little girls dressed all in black,
Set out one Halloween Night,
Several years back.

Linda and Jill and a small dog named Smarty,
Walked to Falls River School,
To a big costume party.

They entered the building and went down the hall,
They saw many spooks,
Some big and some small.

"I'm scared," said Jill. "They all look so mean."
But when she looked back around,
Linda was nowhere to be seen.

"Linda, where are you? Smarty, where did you go?"
Jill screamed out in fear,
And she looked high and low.

She backed up slowly and felt something furry.
She yelled in fear, hit her head on the wall.
When she opened her eyes everything was blurry.

"What happened," she wondered and rubbed her head.
"Where did everyone go?
Have I been sleeping or am I dead?"

Jill never knew what happened during her plight,
On that Halloween night she received such a fright.

Directions

🦇 Choose the characters and setting for a scary story.

🦇 Use these elements to write the story in the form of a poem.

🦇 The poem should be at least seven verses.

🦇 Each verse should consist of three lines, using the ABA rhyming pattern.

🦇 The last verse can use a different pattern.

Thanksgiving Day

Overview

The students will write poetry by compiling a list of things they have to give and incorporating these into a list poem.

Objectives

- Students will brainstorm lists of things they own or personal qualities they possess that they feel are worth giving to someone else.
- Students will rate the list to determine what are the most valuable items.
- Students will create list poems incorporating the most valuable items.

Materials

✓ paper
✓ pens and pencils

Procedure

1. During a 20-minute brainstorming session, students write down at least 20-25 things they have to give to others (preferably intangible items).

2. After the lists have been completed, each student will rate his or her list from the most valuable to the least valuable.

3. The students will take the most valuable items on their lists and use them to write poems that list the items they can give to others. They can add other words as needed.

4. Finally, students should decorate their poems with colorful graphics.

Evaluation

- Participation in a brainstorming session about things worth giving
- A poem that presents tangible and intangible gifts

Sample Poem

The things I have to give:
Warmth,
A caring attitude,
Laughter,
A sense of humor,
The ability to listen,
A little bit of money,
Generosity of spirit,
Lunch on me,
Love,
Kindness,
Spirituality,
A party,
A lovely present,
A cake on your birthday,
Lightness of heart,
A movie and popcorn,
A positive attitude,
A poem,
My favorite seashell,
A watercolor picture,
And best of all,
Loyalty and friendship!
by Karen B.

Winter Holidays

Overview

Students write two verses of poetry that contrast the warm things and the cold things of winter holidays.

Objectives

- Students will reflect on two different sides (the hot and cold) of Christmas or Hanukkah.
- Students will write their ideas in poems.
- Students will design Christmas or Hanukkah fliers or cards to display the poems.

Materials

✓ paper
✓ pens and pencils
✓ construction paper
✓ markers, crayons, paints, or colored pencils
✓ copies of page 92

Procedure

1. To start, have students complete the listing activity on page 92. On one side of the page they will list the hot or warm things associated with Christmas or Hanukkah. On the other side they will list the cold things. Examples of warm or hot things might be a warm fire, hot chocolate on a cold night, the feeling of a loving family. Some examples of things that are cold might be a beautiful snowfall, a case of the flu, a brisk or freezing wind. Ask them to think of figurative as well as literal representations of hot and cold.

2. Once students have filled out their lists, they should use the words to write two verses about the holiday. One of the verses will be about the warm or hot associations and the other will talk about the cold things. The poems may take any form.

3. Once the poems have been written and a final copy typed or neatly handwritten, have students design Christmas or Hanukkah fliers or cards with the poems featured on them.

Evaluation

- Ideas for two different aspects of a holiday
- Poem that describes the hots and colds of Christmas or Hanukkah
- Attractive card or flyer that highlights the poem

Extensions

- Students can write poems about the sounds and smells of Christmas.
- Students can write poems or stories that chronicle each day of Hanukkah.
- Have students write a six-line verse about the warm things of winter and another six-line verse about the cold things of winter.
- Students can read *Winter* by Richard Hughes or *Stopping by the Woods on a Snowy Evening* by Robert Frost.

What things do you think of when you recall winter holidays? Write all the warm associations in the space on the left. Write all the cold associations in the space on the right. Use these words and phrases to write a poem about Christmas or Hanukkah.

Warm Thoughts   Cool Thoughts

_____   _____

_____   _____

_____   _____

_____   _____

_____   _____

_____   _____

_____   _____

_____   _____

_____   _____

_____   _____

_____   _____

_____   _____

92

The Two Sides of Christmas

Cozy winter nights,
  Christmas tree lights blinking like glittering diamonds,
Heavenly heat from a blazing fire,
  Its flickering glow reflected in its surroundings.
 Steaming hot cocoa, gooey, chocolatey goodness,
  Its delicious aroma mesmerizes the senses.
And a wooly afghan slung over a sofa,
  Inviting one to curl up with a book.
It is Christmas Eve,
  Warmth radiates,
  Family and friends gather all around.

Christmas – icy tendrils of bitter winds,
  Rattling the windows and doors.
Sleeping under the woolen blankets,
  People lay shivering in the night.
The cold and lovely snow,
  Fresh-fallen on the yard and house,
  Sparkling in the moonlight.
Christmas presents, looking cold and lonely,
  Bright coverings torn and discarded,
The aftermath of Christmas morning.

Winter Contrasts

Expectation lurks,
Excitement perks,
Christmas is coming.
Carols everywhere,
People show they care,
Preparations are humming.
Decorations resplendent,
Feasts transcendent,
Dreams sugar-pluming.

Rains are soaking,
Umbrellas are poking,
The weather is tiresome.
Pageants staging,
Tempers raging,
People are quarrelsome.
Macy's advertises,
Money vaporizes,
Shopping is tedium.

A Year in Retrospect

Overview

Students stretch their thinking abilities to remember events that occurred in the year just ended, and they write poems that sum up the most important memories of the year. This activity should be given to students on the first day of school after returning from the winter holidays.

Calender

Objectives

- Students will respond to questions about their memories of the previous year.
- Students will prioritize their responses.
- Students will write poems that present the most important events of the year.
- Students will assemble collages that creatively represent the preceding year.

Materials

- ✓ black pens, pencils
- ✓ paper
- ✓ copies of page 95 and 96
- ✓ magazines, old photos, fancy papers
- ✓ scissors
- ✓ glue

Procedure

1. Pass out copies of page 95. Instruct students to work independently and answer as many questions as they possibly can.

2. After students have had an adequate amount of time to work on their own, (approximately 20-30 minutes) discuss students' responses. If they left any questions unanswered, they should fill in the blank spaces at this time.

3. Once the discussion has ended, instruct students to evaluate their answers and select at least the facts, feelings, or issues that they consider the most representative of the year. The questionnaire is just a starting place. Encourage students to incorporate other information about the world, fads, events, pop culture, or their personal events. These items should then be organized into the rough draft of a poem, entitled "It Was a Very _____ Year."

4. Hand out magazines, scissors, and glue and assign students the task of creating a collage to represent the events of the year. Once the poem has been completed and revised, it should be written on top or to the side of the collage.

Evaluation

- A poem that is not in a particular format but incorporates some poetic devices
- The overall quality of the finished collage/poem
- The quality of information presented in the poem
- The creativity of the collage

Extensions

- Students may choose to write an essay about the year's most important events.
- The class may collaborate on a front-page mock-up of a newspaper that incorporates all of the news stories and important information from the past year.

❖ *A Year in Retrospect*   **Directions**

General questions about the last year.

Questions about your own life during the past year.

The last year was_____

1. What three world leaders were most mentioned in the news?

   _____
   _____
   _____

2. What were the two most important news stories of the last year?

   _____
   _____

3. Name two women in the news.

   _____
   _____

   Name two men in the news.

   _____
   _____

4. Name two books that were published or gained popularity.

   _____

1. Name three of the most important events from your life in the past year.

   _____
   _____
   _____

2. Which of these was the most important?

   _____

3. Name two people who had an important impact on your life.

   _____
   _____

4. What was your favorite movie?

   _____

5. What was your favorite song?

   _____

6. What was the most beautiful place you visited? _____

7. In what ways have you changed?

   _____

2001 - It Was a Very Tragic Year

On September 11th, two thousand and one,
The terrorists struck,
And a war had begun.

George "Dubya" Bush, our leader and chief,
Proved to be strong,
As we dealt with our grief.

After 9/11 we developed great pride.
We waved the red, white and blue,
And "Love America" we cried.

In spite of the chaos that was all surrounding.
We went on with our lives,
And that was astounding.

We went to see movies like "Lord of the Rings,"
And we read Harry Potter,
And all sorts of things.

Kids went on to school and did homework too.
They played soccer and danced,
But still they all knew.

That the world was different, in a way,
Due to events
From that fateful day.

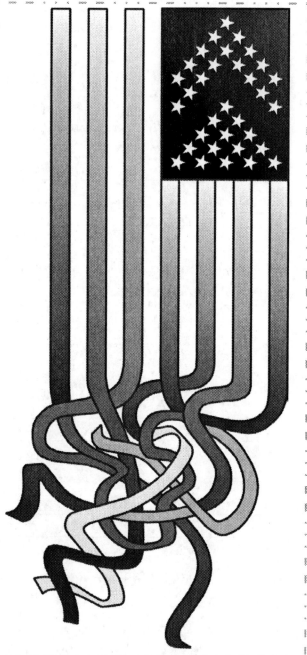

Directions

❋ Fill out the questionnaire about the events of the last year.

❋ Take at least ten feelings or events from the last year and incorporate them into a poem

❋ Your poem should consist of at least ten lines. It may be rhymed or unrhymed.

❋ Give your poem a title like "It Was a Very _____ Year."

A Sense of Spring

Overview

The students will incorporate impressions from all their senses into a poem about Easter or spring.

Objective

- Students will list words or phrases associated with things detected by each of their senses.
- Students will use these ideas to write poems about spring or Easter.
- Students will create spring graphics as borders to the poems.

Materials

✓ paper
✓ pens and pencils
✓ clipboards or notebooks for a field trip to the school campus or a nearby park
✓ markers, crayons, colored pencils or watercolors

Procedure

1. Read the poem "Spring" by Karla Kushkin. Then take students out to the school campus with notebooks and clipboards on a pretty spring day. Allow students to write words or phrases that correspond to input from each of the senses. Use the following questions:
   - Sight - What do you see? List at least five words.
   - Hearing - What are at least five sounds of spring?
   - Smell - What are five smells of spring?
   - Taste - What are five tastes reminiscent of spring?
   - Touch - What are five things you can touch in the spring?
   - Emotions - Describe in one sentence how you feel in the spring.

2. Back in the classroom, have students use these words to write a poem about spring. The poem may take any form.

3. Finally have students decorate the border of a piece of paper and write the poem inside the border.

Evaluation

- Participation in a note-taking field trip
- A spring poem that includes several sensual references
- Attractively decorated border for the poem

Extension

- Have students select only one of the senses and write poems or descriptive paragraphs.

A Sense of Spring

The sights of spring
Multicolored Easter eggs,
Glorious golden sunshine,
Ever-present colors of orange and yellow,
Leafy green trees,
Exquisitely-formed flowers.

The smells of spring
Tantalizing spiciness of barbeque on the grill,
Mustiness of newly turned earth,
Freshness of the air after a soaking rain,
Pungent fragrance of honeysuckle on the vine,
The familiar smell of freshly mowed grass.

The sounds of spring
The sing-song of children's voices,
The solid whack of a ball hitting a bat,
Tree branches whispering in the wind,
Cheerfully chirping birds,
The harmonic buzzing of bees.

The tastes of spring
Smooth and satisfying ice cream cones,
Sweet and juicy strawberries,
Full-of-flavor, fresh tomatoes,
Hearty hamburgers cooked on the grill,
Icy, honey-sweet Popsicles.

A touch of spring
The prickly feel of overgrown grass,
Fresh air gently brushing against your skin,
The warm, gritty beach sand between you toes,
The cool freshness of an air-conditioned house,
The silky, plush-like fur of an Easter bunny.

The emotional feel of a spring day
It makes me feel happy,
As if everything is new and fresh,
Giving us all a sense of hope.

Directions

🌹 What do you see, feel, smell during this time of the year?

🌹 Make a list of everything you experience about this time of year using your five senses.

🌹 Incorporate these ideas into a six-stanza poem in which each of the first five stanzas reflect a different sense. The last stanza will tell how this season makes you feel.

Mother's Day

Overview

Students will fill out a questionnaire to determine how well they know their mothers, and they will write poetry sharing information about their mothers.

Objectives

• Students will complete questionnaires about their mothers.

• Students will compare their answers with their mother's answers.

• Students will create poems that celebrate their mothers' special characteristics.

• Students will decorate their poems.

Materials

✓ paper
✓ pens and pencils
✓ copies of page 101
✓ markers, crayons, colored pencils or watercolors

Procedure

1. Have students fill in the questionnaire on page 101, answering all questions as best they can. The questionnaires are to be starting points to get students thinking about their mothers and also to begin a dialogues with their mothers.

   Note:
   There are many students who do not have a mother in the true sense of the word. Some of them live with stepmothers, grandmothers or in a household of men. This can be very touchy, so it is important that you handle this assignment with care. Tell them to fill in this information based on what they know about a significant female caretaker in their lives.

2. Once the questionnaire has been completed, students should have their mothers complete a similar questionnaire. Students should compare the two sets of answers. Ask students to think about what they learned about their mothers that they did not know before.

3. Each student will use this information to write a poem about his or her mother. The poems may draw from the information on the questionnaires, but students should also incorporate their observations about their mothers and their opinions about what makes them special. The poems can be any length and any format that is appropriate for your students' abilities. One possible format (as shown in the sample poem on page 100) is:
   • Two four-line verses using an AABB rhyming scheme.
   • Each verse begins with a different synonym for the word "mother."
   • The last verse is one line that has five short comments or descriptions.

4. Once the poems are written, have students decorate the pages on which the poems are written. The poems can also be incorporated into Mother's Day cards.

Evaluation

• Completion of the questionnaire

• Understanding of their mothers' special characteristics

• Poem that is aesthetically pleasing and reflects knowledge of the student's mother

Extension

• This activity can be extended to fathers, grandparents, or other relatives. The questionnaire would have to be adapted to fit the gender.

Mother
Kind, gentle,
Transporting, cooking, guiding,
Showing us right from wrong,
Counselor

Dear Mother,
Not only are you very smart,
Not only are you caring,
But you direct me how to act,
Without being overbearing,

Dear Mom,
You always keep the house in shape,
Domestic jobs you juggle,
But you also have another job,
With duties consequential.

Dear Mommy,
Your tastes in clothes are not like mine,
Your music seems so dated,
But as a model there's no better,
You're always my top rated.

My Mother

My Mother …
Beautiful, caring, a health guru,
She's a gourmet cook with eyes of blue.
She's patient and kind when I'm cranky and bad,
And she wipes away my tears when I am sad.

My Mom …
Always there for each of us,
Loving us all without much of a fuss,
Her beaming smile lights up my life,
As she protects me from all pain and strife.

Mama …
Nurturer, healer, good sense of humor, funny and kind.

All About My Mom

Fill out as much information about your mother as you can. Then ask your mother to answer the same questions. Compare your answers to your mother's and see how well you know her.

Full name _____

Favorite color is _____

Favorite flowers _____

Favorite movie _____

_____

Favorite kind of music _____

Favorite singer or musical group _____

_____

Favorite scent _____

Pet peeve _____

Favorite vacation _____

_____

If my mother could go anywhere in the world she would choose to go to

_____

Most embarrassing time _____

_____

_____

Favorite thing to do on a rainy day

_____

_____

Favorite foods _____

_____

_____

Favorite hobby _____

Greatest talent _____

Favorite saying _____

_____

Patriotic Poems

◆ Overview

Students write new national anthems (poems) for their country.

◆ Objectives

- Students will discuss existing patriotic songs.
- Students will evaluate each of the songs, according to their emotional appeal.
- Students will write contemporary national anthems that will evoke feelings of patriotism in people their age.
- Students will design creative patriotic pages to be placed in a booklet of class songs.

◆ Materials

- ✓ paper
- ✓ pens and pencils
- ✓ markers, crayons or watercolor paints
- ✓ copies of existing patriotic songs, including the national anthem

◆ Procedure

1. At the beginning of this lesson, ask students if they know the words to the national anthem. Sing this song together.

2. Give each student a copy of the national anthem, along with music books that contain patriotic songs. Ask them to select three songs that they like the best. Once the results of the top three have been tallied, discuss students' reasons for selecting these particular songs. A set of criteria should then be developed to determine the effectiveness of a good song.

3. Using these student-generated criteria, have each student write a patriotic song. The song should rhyme.

4. Once the songs are written, students should type them on the computer and decorate the pages. Combine all the songs into a class book.

◆ Evaluation

- Participation in a group evaluation of patriotic songs
- A patriotic poem in song form
- Decorated page containing the words to the poem

◆ Sample Poem

My Country

My country, America,
You are so enchanting,
With your blue-crested waters,
And yellow-daisied fields,
Your friendly demeanor,
And many abundant yields.
To live here in freedom,
You make me feel pride.
When I look upon your flag,
As it waves far and wide,
I love how all others,
Try to come to our shores.
They beg to become citizens,
And we open our doors.
My country, America,
You are so enchanting.

A Summer's Day

■ Overview

Students will remember beautiful summer moments in their lives and write descriptive poetry about these moments.

■ Objectives

- Students will complete a webbing activity in which they record summer memories.
- Students will write poems about summer.
- Students will use a series of similes, metaphors and personifications in the poems.

■ Materials

✓ paper
✓ pens and pencils

■ Procedure

1. Before the actual lesson, review simile, metaphor and personification. A **Simile** compares two unlike things using the words "like," "as," and "seems." **Metaphors** imply a direct object-to-object relationship, saying one object is the other object (like Shakespeare's statement that "life is a brief candle"). **Personification** is the technique of giving human qualities to inanimate things. If one referred to "the wind kissing her cheek," the implication is that the wind has the human ability to kiss.

2. Before writing, students will complete a webbing activity for a fond summer memory. They should choose a favorite past event and record their best memories in a thought web. They should have at least three categories that are related to this one summer event. They will use memories of these different aspects of the event to write a poem. The sample on the right shows the beginning of a thought web for recording all the memories related to a parade.

3. Using the ideas from the thought web, they should then write their poems in the following way:

- The memory or event should be divided into three broad categories. For example: a Fourth of July picnic might be divided into the sun, the sky, and the picnic.
- Each category will be described by three lines of poetry that can be rhymed or un-rhymed.
- The first line should be a simile.
- The second line should be a metaphor.
- The third line should be a personification.

■ Evaluation

- Similes, metaphors, and personifications are used correctly in the poems
- Poem that paints a picture of a summer memory with words
- Creatively-written poem that follows a set format

■ Extensions

- Students may write a short story about something that happened to them during a season other than the one they wrote about in the poem.

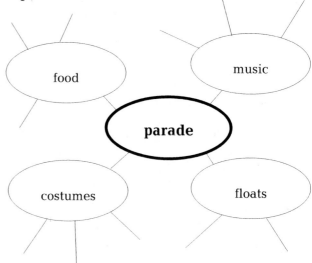

.ample Poem

A Summer Day

The Sky

Its many clouds are like sheep, scattered amongst its
    rolling pastures. (simile)
The sky is a blanket of warmth, a patchwork quilt of
    varying shades of blue and white. (metaphor)
It sleeps lazily, watching the busy world below.
    (personification)

The Sun

Its rays are like fingers, reaching out to comfort
    and thaw the coldest of hearts.
The sun is a bright yellow lemon, bringing forth heat
    and solace and a little sizzle.
At the close of day, it airbrushes the sky with its
    varied palette of colors.

The Picnic

The people are like a flock of birds gathering around
    their food, waiting for their chance to feast.
The children are fun-loving puppies, frolicking in the
    grass.
The leftover food table is sad and lonely, forgotten as
    the day slowly ends.

Directions

- Make a list of things you remember about summer. These memories should be positive ones, reminiscent of happy moments.

- Select one memory and make a thought web.

- Choose three or four broad categories that are most representative of this event and that lend themselves to graphic descriptions. Fill in as many words and phrases as you can that describe this event.

- Use the following pattern to write your poetry:

  Title: (name of the season)
  First category
  - Line 1 - a description that includes a simile
  - Line 2 - a description that includes a metaphor
  - Line 3 - a description that in-cludes a personification

Continue this pattern to write three-line stanzas for two other categories.

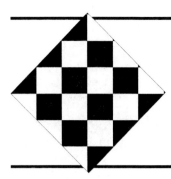

Chapter 6
Side Orders
Time-tested pattern poems

Many of the lessons that have been presented up to this point did not specify a particular poetry format. The lessons presented topics for poems and art that might accompany the finished product, but the type of poem was left open. This section details some of the more common poetry formats. These are to be used in conjunction with the other lessons. Once these are introduced to children, they can choose to employ them in their other writing assignments.

These scrumptious side orders consist of a variety of familiar, time-tested poetry patterns. Some of them may be new to you, but they will nicely fill out your poetry program by providing you with a handy source of reference. The poetry formats presented in this section include:

Clerihew   Limerick
Couplet   Triplet
Quatrain   Cinquain
Diamante   Haiku
Tanka   Sestina
Acrostic   Pantoum
Triolet   Free Verse
Concrete poetry

Clerihew & Limerick

Clerihew

A clerihew is a type of poem that was devised by Edmund Clerihew Bentley. Clerihews consist of four, short lines or two couplets. The rhyming pattern is AABB. It has no definite metrical pattern. A clerihew is usually about a person and pokes fun at the person; in fact, the name of the person is in the first line of the poem. It is important to have information about the subject of the poem that can be incorporated into the poem. The subject's name is at the end of the first line and rhymes with the second line.

Sample Poems

The son of his father, George W. Bush,
Was elected to office after Florida's push.
He faces new challenges each and every day,
The president's job doesn't leave much time to play.

❋ ❋ ❋ ❋

Our teacher, whose name is Ms. Jones,
Speaks in the softest of tones.
We all strain to hear when she speaks,
Granting the silence she seeks.

❋ ❋ ❋ ❋

A lady named Juliette Low,
Founded the Girl Scouts, as you know.
The organization grew over the years,
Helping young girls to work with their peers.

Limerick

Limericks have a long history, dating back to the 18th century. They were popularized, however, by Edward Lear during the late 1800s. A limerick is a poem that consists of five lines, using the rhyming pattern AABBA. Lines one, two and five rhyme and are longer. Lines three and four rhyme with each other and are shorter. Limericks are normally humorous and often tell funny stories. The pattern is:

Line 1 - A	long
Line 2 - A	long
Line 3 - B	short
Line 4 - B	short
Line 5 - A	long

Sample Poems

There was a young lady named Sue,
Who thought she had nothing to do.
Then she looked at her list,
And saw she had missed,
Her English assignment and math paper too.

❋ ❋ ❋ ❋

All eyes were on Archibald Snow,
Whose bobsled was ready to go.
He would win the big race,
If he stayed with the pace,
And didn't get caught down below.

❋ ❋ ❋ ❋

There was an old man of Cape Horn,
Who wished he had never been born,
So he sat on a chair
Till he died of despair,
That dolorous man of Cape Horn.
    Edward Lear

Couplet, Triplet & Quatrain

◆ Couplet

A couplet is a verse composed of two lines that are usually rhymed. Couplets can be simple or complex, and the length of each line can be determined by the writer. Longer poems can be written using a series of couplets. Many nursery rhymes employ combinations of couplets. When young people write couplets, they should make sure their lines make sense as well as rhyme.

Sample Poems

I have a new dress,
But my hair is a mess.

Although my money is in limited supply,
I'll shop 'til there's nothing left to buy.

Nature has all the creatures it needs,
Including the multi-legged centipedes.

◆ Triplet

Triplets are poems consisting of three lines that can either rhyme or not. If they rhyme, there are several different patterns. The first sample below uses an AAA pattern, and the second sample uses an ABA pattern. Like couplets, triplets can be found in many nursery rhymes. When combined into longer poems, each three-line set is called a stanza.

Sample Poems

There was a very sad little boy,
Who cried when he broke his toy,
But Mom's hugs brought him comfort and joy.

✳ ✳ ✳ ✳

A magical thing happened one day,
When the loveliest tree in the wood,
Bent down its branches to play.

◆ Quatrain

Quatrains are four-lined poems that are usually rhymed. They can be used as separate verses in longer poems, in which case they are called stanzas. Some of the rhyming patterns that are commonly used are:

AABB   AAAA
ABAB   ABCC
ABCB (this is the most common pattern).

Most nursery rhymes are children's poems are written in quatrains with easily distinguishable rhyming patterns. Studying a few samples will give students an appreciation for these rhyme patterns. In the samples below the rhyming patterns are noted to the right of each line.

Sample Poems

A caterpillar ambled onto a branch,	A
And began to spin a cocoon.	B
For many a day it stayed submerged,	C
Then a butterfly magically emerged.	C

✳ ✳ ✳ ✳

Good people all, of every sort,	A
Give ear unto my song;	B
And if you find it wondrous short,	A
It cannot hold you long.	B
Oliver Goldsmith	

✳ ✳ ✳ ✳

Chang McTang McQuarter Cat,	A
Is one part this and one part that.	A
One part is yowl, one part is purr.	B
One part is scratch, one part is fur.	B
John Ciardi	

✳ ✳ ✳ ✳

Oh beautiful for spacious skies,	A
For amber waves of grain,	B
For purple mountains majesties,	C
Above the fruited plain.	B
Katharine Lee Bates	

Cinquain & Diamante

◾ Cinquain

A cinquain is a pattern poem that consists of five unrhymed lines. Each line must follow a prescribed format. Originally, cinquains were written with a strict syllabication format (no word count restrictions). Because this format was difficult for elementary students to master, the format was altered and cinquains are now usually presented to elementary and middle school students with only the five-line, word count format, but with no syllable count. The format below shows the syllable count, should you choose to teach it this way; but you may also present the easier structure with word counts. Either format is acceptable. The pattern for these poems is:

Line 1 - a noun   *(2 syllables)*

Line 2 - two adjectives that describe the noun   *(4 syllables)*

Line 3 - three action words ("ing" words)   *(6 syllables)*

Line 4 - a phrase about the topic that is descriptive or conveys feeling   *(8 syllables)*

Line 5 - a word that renames the subject of the poem or is related to it   *(2 syllables)*

Samples

without syllabication

Robins
Cute, perky
Flying, swooping, playing
Grubbing for little worms
Red-breasts

★ ★ ★ ★

with syllabication

My room,
Clothes everywhere,
Books scattered on the floor,
A part of me wants to clean up,
Some day.

◾ Diamante

A diamante is a seven-line poem in the shape of a diamond. It begins with a one-word noun and ends with a word that is the opposite of that noun. The pattern is:

Line 1 - The topic of the poem (a noun)

Line 2 - Two adjectives that describe the topic

Line 3 - Three action words ("ing" or "ed" words)

Line 4 - Four words, changing topics – two words that describe the subject and two words that describe the noun in the last line

Line 5 - Three action words ("ing" or "ed" words) that refer to the new topic

Line 6 - Two adjectives that describe the noun in the last line

Line 7 - A noun that is the opposite of the first topic

Samples

Puppies
Lovable, Adorable
Chewing, Running, Jumping
Frisky, Not-housebroken, Obedient, Loyal
Sleeping, Heeling, Listening
Well-mannered, Wonderful
Dogs

★ ★ ★ ★

Moon,
Pale, Pearl-like,
Reflecting, Revolving, Waning
Peaceful, Desolate, Volatile, Fiery
Blazing, Fueling, Erupting, Glowing
Brilliant, Stellar
Sun

Haiku & Tanka

Haiku

Haiku (pronounced hi-koo) poems are short Japanese poems that are very descriptive and paint a picture with a few words. These three-lined poems consist of seventeen syllables. They are unrhymed and have no particular metrical pattern. They do, however, describe one subject, usually something in nature. The purpose of these poems is to create a brief, vivid picture for the reader. The pattern is:

Line 1 - 5 syllables
Line 2 - 7 syllables
Line 3 - 5 syllables

Sample Poems

A crystal-clear lake,
Serene and independent,
Ripples in the wind.

★ ★ ★ ★

A glorious sky,
Blue painted with rosy peach,
Like nature's palette.

★ ★ ★ ★

Soaring red tail hawk,
Taking aim then nose-diving,
Predator on wings.

Tanka

A tanka is similar to a haiku, but it gives the writer two more lines to develop his or her thoughts. The tanka consists of 31 syllables and five lines. The first three lines are called *haiku* and are considered the starting verse. The last two lines are called *ageku* and are the conclusion. The format is:

Line 1.......5 syllables
Line 2.......7 syllables
Line 3.......5 syllables
Line 4.......7 syllables
Line 5.......7 syllables

Sample Poems

A croaking tree frog
Can be heard in the evening
Leading the night's choir
Joining the chirping crickets
And the whining mosquitoes.

★ ★ ★ ★

Serene, babbling brook,
Running carefree where you want,
Plunging down steep slopes,
Meandering though meadows,
Singing nature's lullaby.

★ ★ ★ ★

A beautiful rose,
Basking in the morning dew,
In regal splendor,
Tall, in solitary joy,
Stretching to greet the sunshine.

Triolet & Sestina

■ Triolet

The triolet, like the sestina and several other forms of French-derived poetry, is a form of rhyming poetry that has lines that repeat. These forms of poetry, like some forms of music, use the repetition and rearrangement of lines to add structure to the poem. The triolet is the simplest of these types of poems. It consists of eight lines. The second line is repeated twice (as lines 2 and 8), and the first line is repeated three times (lines, 1, 4, and 7). This poem is easier than the sestina and should probably be introduced before studying the longer and more complicated sestina. The pattern for the triolet is:

line 1 - A
line 2 - B
line 3 - A
line 4 - A - repeat of line 1
line 5 - A
line 6 - B
line 7 - A - repeat of line 1
line 8 - B - repeat of line 2

Sample Poem

A new car can be such a lot of fun,
With smooth, cool leather, it smells so good,
And you can be sure that it will run,
A new car can be such a lot of fun.
It sparkles like diamonds in the noonday sun,
From the bumper in back to the tip of its hood,
A new car can be such a lot of fun,
With smooth, cool leather, it smells so good.

■ Sestina

The sestina has a rather complicated poetic format, but it can be simple for students to learn. You will get much better results if your students write a collaborative sestina before they try it as an independent activity.

A sestina is usually unrhymed and consists of 39 lines, broken into six stanzas of six lines each, and a seventh stanza of just three lines. There is an exact pattern to these poems.

Students begin this poem by selecting six words to be used as the ending words of each of the six lines in each stanza. These words will be repeated in all of the stanzas but in a different order each time, so it is very important to select six words that connect in some way. The seventh stanza will have a slightly different pattern. The pattern is:

- **First stanza** - Each of the six lines will end with one of the six preselected words. Number the words and write a key at the top of the paper. The pattern for the first stanza will be 123456. Lines should be written to match the ending words. The challenge is to make the lines fit with the words.

- **Second stanza** - The same ending words will be used in this stanza, but the order will be changed. The new order will be *615243*. Once again the students must write lines (new ones) to fit the ending words.

- **Third stanza** - The new pattern for the ending words will be *364125*.

- **Fourth stanza** - The pattern is *532614*.

- **Fifth stanza** - The pattern is *451362*.

- **Sixth stanza** - The pattern is *246531*.

- **Seventh stanza** - The last stanza follows a different format and has only three lines. In each of the last three lines there are two numbered words, and the order is the same as in the first stanza: that is, *123456*. The first line will contain word 1 in the sentence somewhere and end with word 2. The second line will contain word 3 and will end with word 4. The last line will contain word 5 and will end with 6.

The Lake Sestina

Looking out on its crystal, clear **waters,**
I watched the lake shimmering in the last radiant rays of **sunset.**
Looming like giant shadows were the **trees,**
And laughing their silly songs, a devoted pair of **loons,**
Were heard in the deepening **darkness,**
As we gently paddled the small, creaky **boat.**

As we neared the shore we slowed the **boat,**
And listened as a large bass splashed in the nearby **waters,**
Off in the distance we could see a light in the **darkness,**
As it blended with the purples and reds of the darkening **sunset,**
We saw the shadowy forms of the swimming **loons,**
As they propelled their bodies toward the safety of the **trees.**

The sound of the winged bats were heard above the **trees,**
And they could be seen flying closely above our small **boat,**
It was hard to distinguish their noises from those of the **loons,**
Or all of the other creatures moving about the placid **waters,**
A reddish hue was all that could be seen of the remaining **sunset,**
As the earth was plunged into **darkness.**

The nocturnal beasts took over in the **darkness,**
As they scrambled rapidly from tree to other **tree,**
Their bodies in playful readiness for the last of the **sunset,**
Their yellow eyes could be seen as they watched the **boat,**
As it stealthily skimmed the surface of the lake **waters,**
Listening for the comforting noises of the **loons.**

The cheerful banter of the pair of **loons,**
Could be heard but not seen in the **darkness,**
And the light from the moon could be seen reflected on the **waters,**
And shining sporadically through the branches of the tall pine **trees,**
Its reflected light bounced off the hull of the **boat,**
And mingled with the waning rays of the **sunset.**

The fading of the lovely **sunset,**
Made us lose sight of our precious **loons,**
We couldn't see them from our vantage point in the **boat,**
And everything was more difficult because of the intense **darkness,**
The creepy shadows of the towering **trees,**
Were like monsters reaching out in the reflection of the **waters.**

The beautiful lakeshore **waters** and the vanquished **sunset,**
Lay amidst the majestic, sweet-smelling pine **trees,** and the last sounds of the **loons**
Are heard as the inky **darkness** settles in, and we head for home in our trusty **boat.**

                Connie H. Weaver

Acrostic & Pantoum

Acrostic

Acrostic poetry is written by choosing words or phrases that describe a topic and start with the letters that spell the topic. The topic of the poem can be a person, place, characteristic or thing. The topic is written vertically. Then words are chosen that start with the letters in each line. Lines can be rhymed or unrhymed. They can be single words, statements or questions. When finished, the first letter in each line spells a word, the subject of the poem, and the lines describe this topic.

Sample Acrostic

M any animals swimming through the deep,
A wakening in the shallows,
R ays, whales, eels and sharks,
I ntermingling with the lesser ones,
N o humans in this underwater world,
E xcept for the occasional deep-sea diver.

L ife in the ocean is busy, full of movement,
I ncreasingly turbulent,
F ull of mystery and drama,
E nergetic and beautiful!

Pantoum

The pantoum format had its origins in Malaysia. It consists of a series of interrelated four-line stanzas. The second and fourth lines of each stanza become the first and third lines in the following stanza. In the final stanza the first line of the first stanza will be used as the fourth (last) line of the last stanza, and the third line of the first stanza becomes the second line of the last stanza. The rhyming pattern is:

Lines 1-4	ABAB
Lines 5-8	BCBC
Lines 9-12	CDCD
Lines 13-16	DEDE
Lines 17-20	EFEF
Lines 21-24	FGFG
Lines 25-28 (last stanza)	GAGA

Poems can be shorter than the sample (28 lines). Start by having students write shorter poems, choosing lines that make sense in two different places and methodically building a pattern. It is also easier to write a poem that is a description than one that tells a story.

Sample Pantoum

A Mountain View

Driving through the desert land,
The view from the train was boring,
The sights we saw were bleak and bland,
And many folks were snoring.

The view from the train was boring,
As we hurtled through the day,
And many folks were snoring,
There was nothing much to say.

As we hurtled through the day,
We watched with hopeful eyes,
There was nothing much to say,
And many people heaved great sighs.

We watched with hopeful eyes,
Waiting for a subtle change,
And many people heaved great sighs,
While looking for a mountain range.

Waiting for a subtle change,
Everyone stared and waited,
While looking for a mountain range,
We watched with our breaths baited.

Everyone stared and waited,
At last!...the first majestic peak,
We watched with our breaths baited,
No one dared to even speak.

At last! The first majestic peak,
The sights we saw were bleak and bland,
No one dared to even speak
Driving through the desert land.

Free Verse & Concrete Poems

◆ Free Verse

The one form of poetry that does not follow a definite pattern, but is used frequently in the samples of this text, is free verse. Free verse is poetry without end rhyme or meter, though it may employ other poetic devices. It is broken into short words, phrases, and sentences. Walt Whitman and Dylan Thomas employed this type of writing; and in some languages, all poetry has been written as free verse.

Free verse differs from blank verse, which also is unrhymed but employs iambic pentameter. Like free verse, blank verse does not use formal stanza units.

Because it is free of the more formal rules the other forms of poetry follow, it is easy for children to write. This form of poetry can be used in many of the assignments in this book.

Sample Poems

Watermelon

Big and green,
Reddish, pink and juicy within,
Black seeds throughout,
Cool,
Delicious,
And sweet,
Relief on a hot summer day.

★ ★ ★ ★

The Maple Leaf

Dancing happily on its limb,
Like a small child playing,
Arms spread wide.
Green,
Then red and yellow,
Sometimes orange,
And finally brown.
It spirals downward,
Covering the winter ground,
Like a warm, woolen blanket.

◆ Concrete Poetry

Concrete poetry also does not follow a specific rhyming or syllabic pattern. Sometimes called picture poems or shape poems, it combines poetic writing and drawing. The form that the poem is written in mirrors the topic of the poem. That is, the poem can follow the outline of the object, can fill a shape that is the subject of the poem, or can use the way words are written on the page to form an image. Though concrete poems have been around for hundreds of years, this type of poetry reached its peak in the 1960s and 1970s. It is a good technique to use with reticent writers or when you want to incorporate art without doing a full-on art project.

Sample Poems

Bells,
Pealing, tolling,
Exclaiming cheer,
Sounding celebration.
Boisterously crying out,
Soft tinkles and loud clangs,
High trills and annoying jangles,
Bells.

★ ★ ★ ★

The waves capture my attention.
Undulating in perfect rhythm,
Up on tip toes then slouching low.
Raising their white-haired heads
like a snake ready to strike.
Then crashing at my feet.

Lessons Using Pattern Poems

Clerihew

- Choose characters from the comic strips or cartoon shows and write clerihew poems about these characters.
- Assign students to write clerihew poems about people they have studied in history.

Couplets

- Give students a couplet and let them write a second couplet to complete the first two lines.

Triplets

- Give students the first two lines from nursery rhymes. Ask them to supply the third line and then write a second triplet to finish the rhyme.
  Example:
  Jack and Jill
  Went up a hill,
  (add line 3)
  (add three more lines to complete the poem)

Cinquain

- Using the form of cinquains that assigns syllables for each line, have students write double cinquain poems. These are poems in which the number of syllables for each line is twice that of a regular cinquain. The syllable count is:
  line 1 - 4 syllables
  line 2 - 8 syllables
  line 3 - 12 syllables
  line 4 - 16 syllables
  line 5 - 4 syllables

Quatrain

- Have one person write two lines of a poem that uses an ABAB or an ABCB format. Have students trade papers and complete the poems.

Pantoum

- Have students start by writing a short poem, just three stanzas. These will have the pattern ABAB - BCBC - CACA.

Diamante

- Have students write diamante poems using one of the following pairs of opposites:

night - day	dark - light
winning losing	success - failure
honor - infamy	comedy - tragedy
summer - winter	summer - winter
virtue - vice	harmony - discord
teacher - student	birth - death
fiction - reality	beginner - expert
ridicule - praise	truth - falseness

- Write diamante poems to move from one era or historic event to another.

Tanka

- Ask students to write a couple of haiku poems. Put them away for a week. When you give the poems back, ask students if they can add two lines to any of the poems to turn them into tanka poems. They should only add lines that will enhance and finish the poems, not ones that will seem tacked on.

Acrostic

- Have students write acrostic poems for their Mother's Day poetry.
- Have students write acrostic poems about themselves, friends, or characters from books they are reading.

Triolet

- Have students write triolet poems that are school songs or cheers.
- Give students a line from a previously published poem. Use this line to build a new poem.

Haiku

- Pass out pictures of outdoor scenes from magazines, cards or calendars. Write haiku poems about these nature scenes.

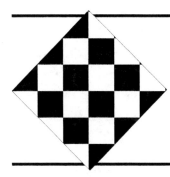

Chapter 6
À la Carte Items
Ideas for Sharing Poetry Orally

This section consists of ideas for sharing poetry via poetry reading nights where students share their poetry with parents and classmates and through oral presentations and poetry slams. While many of the poems that children write are created in the privacy of their journals, it is worthwhile to offer students a chance to share their work with others. In addition to publishing or posting their poems, oral poetry reading gives them the opportunity to practice public speaking and also to provide the emphasis in their poems that they had envisioned when they were written.

In this section of the book, you will find information on:

- Staging a poetry night
- Student guidelines for reading poetry
- Staging poetry slams

Poetry Night

This section offers guidance in producing a poetry reading event. While it is assumed that you will find many opportunities to share students' poetry on an ongoing basis in the classroom, setting aside a special night when students can present their work to parents makes their writings more important. It gives them the motivation to rework their writings to produce the best poems, and it presents the opportunity to practice public speaking. While the instructions in this section are for an evening event that includes parents, you can use the ideas to stage smaller daytime events, perhaps with other classes.

◆ Preparing Students and Student Work

- Ask each student to keep a poetry portfolio that contains a large variety of assignments and includes rough drafts as well as finished products

- Immerse students in a study of great poetry from writers such as Shel Silverstein, T.S. Eliot, Elizabeth Barrett Browning, Edgar Allan Poe, Walt Whitman, Robert Browning, Emily Dickinson, Robert Frost, Henry Wadsworth Longfellow, Edna St. Vincent Millay, and Lord Byron. Have them collect great poetry and allow them time to read some of their favorites to the class. This should be a year-long practice.

- Publish student work throughout the year in a variety of ways, such as hanging it on the classroom walls, placing poems in unusual places and submitting student work for publication in school newsletters or magazines that specialize in children's writing.

- In the spring of the year, each student should select a favorite (preferably short) poem to be used for reading at the poetry sharing event. Some of the students may choose to present their poems as songs accompanied by music. Others may wish to use a more dramatic approach by acting out their poems.

- Encourage the students to memorize their poems because their delivery at the microphone will be much more effective and entertaining if they know the poems by heart. Occasionally there are those students who are terrified of standing before an audience without a piece of paper in their hands. Encourage them to try saying their poems without the piece of paper, but don't force the issue if they appear to be extremely concerned.

- Students may opt to take on the additional roles of masters of ceremonies, musicians, ushers, wait staff, decoration committee members, poetry book editors, and any other positions that are needed for the big event.

Setting the Stage

One way to make your poetry night more dramatic is to make the area for your poetry reading reminiscent of the coffeehouses that were popular during the 60's and 70's. The following suggestions will make your poetry reading setting more realistic, successful and entertaining:

- Use a brick wall as a backdrop for the poetry readings. If you don't have one in your school, let your students draw bricks on large, white bulletin board paper and hang it at the back of the staging area.

- It is not a good idea to use a large stage in an auditorium. The event needs a cozier area that is not so intimidating.

- Use a raised platform for the stage. It doesn't have to be large, just big enough to hold a stool and a student or two.

- Hang posters to decorate the area. These can be purchased or designed by the more artistic students.

- To create a more informal, relaxing atmosphere you can have the audience sit at tables instead of rows of chairs. Ask students to bring card tables from home and cover these tables in cheap gingham cloth. Have the students make table decorations.

- Cover the walls with student poetry and artwork.

- A microphone should be set up on the stage. If you have a karaoke machine, it can be used as both a cassette player and an extra microphone.

- Add to the ambiance of your poetry reading by serving light snacks and beverages.

The Big Night

On the day of the big event, keep the following details in mind:

- Assign one boy and one girl the jobs of masters of ceremonies. These students should begin the festivities by welcoming their guests with prepared speeches.

- Ask teachers or students to run the spotlight and the cassette or CD player.

- Plan for a variety of music to be played throughout the evening.

- Remember to have a cleanup crew ready as soon as the program is finished.

Tips for Reading Poetry

⭐ Memorize your poem. Even though you created it, you must become totally familiar with each verse.

⭐ Practice saying your poem, both with and without the written copy in front of you.

⭐ Connect with your audience by looking directly at them. If you get nervous or forget some of the words, focus on the friendly faces looking back at you.

⭐ Speak loudly and distinctly. It is not necessary, however, to scream or yell your words.

⭐ Stand up straight and tall. Your posture should show the proper body language. If you slouch, you will not appear confident.

⭐ Read your poem with emotion. Show the feelings that went into writing it.

⭐ Emphasize certain words by saying them a little louder or with more enthusiasm. Pause where it is appropriate and vary the pace of your speaking if it will add emphasis to your poem.

Poetry Slam

What is a Poetry Slam?

"Slamming" originated in the mid-1980's when Marc Smith, a poet from Chicago, came up with the idea to entertain Sunday customers at a bar called the Green Mill. To spice up the event, he randomly selected judges from the audience to rate the poems. It has taken several years for this phenomenon to catch on, but it is gradually gaining popularity. Most of the poetry slams are conducted in adult venues only, but the rules can be adapted to fit the needs of children in middle school.

A poetry slam is similar to a coffeehouse "open mic" event, but there are some differences. Poetry slams have the following characteristics:

- A poetry slam is a competition in which original poetry is performed before an audience and judges.

- The poetry is performed in a creatively dramatic way by both individuals and teams.

The Rules

- Students may enter the competition as individuals, as well as members of a team.

- No props, costumes, or musical accompaniments are allowed.

- Participants are allowed up to three minutes to present their poems. Penalties are assessed for going overtime.

- Poems can be about any appropriate subject.

The Procedure

- Divide the class into teams of four members each. Ask each team member to submit several original poems to the group. The groups should then decide which poems will be presented during a bout. Each bout allows a team to have four poetry performances (one for each person on the team). These four performances are not necessarily done by each individual on the team. Some of them may be better suited to present as a duo, trio, or whole team performance. The team must come to a consensus as to how they want to present the four selected poems.

- If a student's poem is not selected for performance, that student will still have the option of presenting his own poetry in an individual competition that will be scored separately from the team competition.

The Agenda

- **Bout 1** - Have all of the teams present their four poems. The two top teams will then compete in Bout 2.

- **Bout 2** - Choices have to be made at this point. The winning teams may wish to present the poems differently. For example, if someone presented a poem in the whole-group format in bout one, they may decide that it would be more effective to present it with only two people in bout two. They may also substitute a poem not used in bout one for one of their four poems. Only one poem can be substituted, and it is clearly a gamble to do so, because it has not been tested on the judges.

- **Bout 3** - This is the individual competition round. Individuals may present original poems (no less that four verses) that have not been used in any of the other two bouts. Scoring is based on originality, presentation, and creativity of the performance. Students must present their own poetry, not that of other students.

119

Optional Bouts

- **Impromptu Poems** - Give the teams a pre-printed list of words and a short amount of time to think of a poem, and then three minutes to perform two haikus or limericks. These may be performed by individuals and or members of the group together.

- **Grab Bag Magnetic Poetry** - All four team members come to the stage and pull 40 magnetic poetry pieces out of a bag. They are given five minutes to create a poem and place it on a magnetic board.

- **Pass the Poem** - This activity is both a fun and creative way to do teamwork improvisation. Someone (one of the judges) calls out a subject that has been randomly drawn from a box that contains topics written on pieces of paper. All four team members participate by standing in a line and saying one word at a time. The tricky part is that their words have to form a rhyming poem. They must continue for a period of three minutes and create verse after verse until their time is up.

Scoring

Points range from 1-10, with 10 being the highest. Points are based on the choice of poetry, the presentation, the quality of the poems, and the ability of the team to work together. The team with the most points wins.